TWAYNE'S WORLD AUTHORS SERIES
A Survey of the World's Literature

Sylvia E. Bowman, Indiana University
GENERAL EDITOR

GERMANY

Ulrich Weisstein, Indiana University
EDITOR

Eduard Mörike

(TWAS 72)

TWAYNE'S WORLD AUTHORS SERIES (TWAS)

The purpose of TWAS is to survey the major writers
—novelists, dramatists, historians, poets, philosophers,
and critics—of the nations of the world. Among the
national literatures covered are those of Australia,
Canada, China, Eastern Europe, France, Germany,
Greece, India, Italy, Japan, Latin America, New Zea-
land, Poland, Russia, Scandinavia, Spain, and the
African nations, as well as Hebrew, Yiddish, and
Latin Classical literatures. This survey is comple-
mented by Twayne's United States Authors Series
and English Authors Series

The intent of each volume in these series is to present
a critical-analytical study of the works of the writer;
to include biographical and historical material that
may be necessary for understanding, appreciation,
and critical appraisal of the writer; and to present all
material in clear, concise English—but not to vitiate
the scholarly content of the work by doing so.

Eduard Mörike

by HELGA SLESSAREV

University of Cincinnati

Twayne Publishers, Inc.   ::   New York

Preface

The scope of this book, the arrangement of the material, and the method of interpretation were determined by two factors inherent in the task of writing about Eduard Mörike for American readers. We are to discuss a poet whose achievement, especially in the realm of poetry, equals that of the finest lyricists of other nations. Yet we have to begin with a very elementary introduction to the poet and his work, since both are still unknown to wide circles in this country.

There seemed to be only one way of obtaining both objectives: to let the poet himself speak as much as possible. But his voice cannot reach the reader directly; translation has to be employed as a medium. The question was: What approach in translating would best serve as a basis for the discussion of Mörike's poetic achievement, a free one stressing the content and mood of the poems or one that would follow the original closely, trying to imitate the rhyme scheme and the rhythm? Since Mörike's greatness rests in the perfect harmony of content and form he achieved in his poetry, form appeared as an important basis for interpretation and had to receive prime consideration.

After a close reading of the texts, we will proceed to a discussion of form and content. In the case of the prose works, one will find a constant interspersing of summaries of content with commentaries. These include references to pertinent biographical data and to the scholarly discussions of the particular texts up to the present. Attention is focused on the highlights of the works which may be of special interest to the reader of our time.

In preparing the manuscript, I received invaluable help from Professors Edwin H. Zeydel and Bayard Quincy Morgan, who made many suggestions, especially concerning the translations. I am also very grateful to David Kevorkian for improving the style and clarity of the manuscript. A grant from the Charles Phelps Taft Fund enabled me to do some of the work in Germany during the summer of 1966.

EDUARD MÖRIKE

Contents

EDUARD MÖRIKE

by

HELGA SLESSAREV

This volume presents to the American public one of Germany's foremost lyricists. After he had long been admired in smaller circles of initiated readers, Mörike is today considered a great master of the German language. It appears that only now can we fully appreciate the depth of his experiences of Time and Love revealed by his apparently simple works. The imagery of Mörike's nature poems and his renderings of the moment of inspiration lead to the very source of lyrical poetry.

Mrs. Slessarev introduces a large number of Mörike's poems by translating some and analyzing the stylistic qualities of many. She often compares the poems with earlier versions unveiling to us the creative process which led to their perfection. While Mörike pretended that poetry came to him solely by inspiration, this study stresses the artistry of the poet whose feeling for metre, modulation, and rhythm was unfailing.

The second part of the book is concerned with Mörike's prose. Since little of this is translated, besides the novella *Mozart on the Way to Prague*, Mrs. Slessarev combines literary evaluation with introductions to the contents of the narratives. The reader finds himself involved in Mörike's novel *Nolten the Painter* with its complex motivation, fascinated by Mozart's genius as it appears in the novella, or entertained by Mörike's delightful fairy tales. Students may find the discussions of structure and genre especially helpful.

Chronology

1804   On September 8, Eduard Friedrich Mörike is born in Ludwigsburg. His father is the physician Karl Friedrich Mörike, whose ancestors had come to Württemberg from Brandenburg in the late seventeenth century. Mörike's mother is Charlotte Dorothea Beyer, the daughter of a minister. Eduard Mörike is the third of seven living children. He attends the so-called Latin school in Ludwigsburg.

1817   After the death of the father, the family moves to Stuttgart. Eduard receives guidance from his uncle Georgii, who sends him to the *Gymnasium illustre*.

1818   Mörike enters the preparatory school in Urach. He meets Wilhelm Hartlaub, Johannes Mährlen, and Wilhelm Waiblinger, reads Calderón, Shakespeare, Jean Paul, Novalis, and Goethe. Early love for his cousin Klara Neuffer.

1822   Mörike becomes a student of theology at the "Stift" in Tübingen.

1823   He meets Maria Meyer. Close friendship with Waiblinger and Ludwig Bauer.

1824   Death of his brother August. Separation from Maria Meyer.

1826   The theological examination concludes his studies. Beginning of the eight years of wandering from one parish in Württemberg to another as an assistant of country parsons.

1827   Death of his sister Luise. Mörike takes a leave.

1828   He becomes a writer for the *Damenzeitung* in Stuttgart.

1829   Return to the curacy. Love for Luise Rau.

1832   *Nolten the Painter* is published.

1833   End of the engagement to Luise Rau.

1834   Mörike becomes the vicar of Cleversulzbach. Lives with his mother and sister Klara. Visits Justinus Kerner, David Friedrich Strauss, and Hartlaub. "Lucie Gelmeroth" published in the almanac *Urania* under the title "Miss Jenny Harrower."

1836   "The Treasure."

1838   First edition of his *Poems.*

1839   *Iris.* A collection containing "The Treasure," "The Rainbrothers," "The Last King of Orplid," "Lucie Gelmeroth," "The Farmer and His Son."

1840   Translations: *Anthology of Classical Poetry.*

1841   Mörike's mother dies.

1843   Mörike goes into retirement.

1844   He and his sister move, first to Schwäbisch-Hall then to Mergentheim, where they meet Margarete von Speeth.

1846   "The Idyl from Lake Constance."

1848   Second edition of *Poems,* enlarged.

1851   Mörike marries Margarete von Speeth. They move to Stuttgart. Mörike teaches at the High School Katharinenstift.

1852   "The Stuttgart[er] Hutzelmännlein."

1853   "The Hand of Jezerte."

1855   Mörike contributes translations of idyls by Theocritus to Notter's edition. His first daughter Fanny born. Theodor Storm comes for a visit.

1856   "Mozart on the Way to Prague." Third edition of *Poems,* enlarged.

1857   His second daughter, Marie, born.

1863   Friendship with Moritz von Schwind. Vacation in Bebenhausen.

1864   *Anacreon and the So-Called Anacreontics.*

1866   Retirement from the Katharinenstift.

1867   Fourth edition of *Poems,* enlarged.

1873   Separation from Gretchen.

1875   Mörike dies on June 4.

CHAPTER 1

The Life of the Poet

EDUARD MÖRIKE was born in Ludwigsburg near Stuttgart in southwestern Germany on September 8, 1804. The atmosphere of Ludwigsburg was quite different then from the one that another great German poet, Friedrich Schiller, must have experienced in the 1760's. During Schiller's time, the town became transformed from a place of temporary sojourn for the dukes of Württemberg into the main residence of Duke Charles Eugene, who moved there from Stuttgart in 1764 because he was at odds with the citizens of his capital. The population of Ludwigsburg soon rose to 11,000. The town was filled with craftsmen, soldiers, and courtiers, all eager to fulfill the ruler's desire for entertainment. The spacious and lavishly decorated baroque castle, which had been built earlier in the century, was a splendid background for this prince. He now added the mark of his own will by enlarging the town around it. It was this ruler's will against which young Friedrich Schiller had to measure his own strength. He left Württemberg to follow his poetical inclinations rather than submit to Charles Eugene's wishes concerning his professional goals.

Two generations later, at the time of Mörike's birth, the grandeur and vitality had long since deserted the town. When Charles Eugene returned to Stuttgart in 1775, the population of Ludwigsburg had dropped to 4,000. There was no longer a need to protect a young, sensitive mind from the impressions of a frivolous court, as Schiller's parents had tried to do. Eduard Mörike was free to roam in the beautifully landscaped park surrounding the castle and in the country beyond the city gates.

From the beginning, Mörike's mind seemed to take ample nourishment from these surroundings and from the everyday experiences in his family. He was the third living child. His father was a well-educated man and the leading physician of the town. Eduard was followed by three brothers and in 1816 by his sister Klara, the companion of his later years. The family life was gay and happy. Frequent excursions to relatives in other towns of Swabia afforded young Mörike a close acquaintance with his native country.

The landscape of Württemberg is dominated by two mountain ranges, the Black Forest in the West and the Swabian Alb stretching through the center of the country from the Southwest to the Northeast. From the corner in the Southwest, where the Black Forest and the Swabian Alb meet, the river Neckar flows northward to empty eventually into the Rhine. And south of the Swabian Alb the Danube runs through the country from Southwest to Northeast. Further south of this river, Württemberg continues as far as Lake Constance. Traveling from Ludwigsburg the Mörikes thus could choose between the gentler hills toward the North or the rugged slopes of the Swabian Alb in the South over which the cold winds sweep in the winter. Later in life, Mörike made visits to the Danube and Lake Constance, but his trips never took him farther from his native country than to Munich and northern Switzerland.

In 1815 Mörike's father suffered a stroke which impaired his speech and his mental powers. The deep shock caused by seeing the change in the previously strong and active man turned the boy's thoughts to a more serious side of life. The idyllic childhood was over, and two years later, after the father's death, the family split up for lack of financial support. At this crucial moment, Eduard's uncle Georgii offered him a home in Stuttgart.

Eberhard von Georgii was a representative of the wealthy and enlightened middle class of Württemberg that reflected the period's love of the arts and, proud of its privileges and traditions, played an important role in public affairs. Georgii admired the ancient Latin poets and shared this appreciation with his nephew. The city high school, the *Gymnasium illustre,* further broadened Eduard's humanistic education. His course of study could have led to other professions, but the family decided to set a definite goal for the sensitive boy: that of becoming a clergyman.

At this time there existed in Württemberg a number of schools which were formerly run by monasteries. After the secularization of church territories, however, they had been taken over by the state and offered a free education to future Protestant ministers. Admission depended on passing an examination, for which Eduard prepared during the year he stayed in his uncle's house. He did not pass the examination but was still admitted because of his good character and the impoverished situation of his family.

We may ask: was this really the best path for a boy of fourteen who was given to daydreaming and preferred walks in the open air to the rigid discipline of the study hall? Or would he have been strong enough to shape his own fate as a poet without the small but sure income of a country parson? Schiller had tried an independent career and had undermined his health very early. It is true that of the generation before Mörike three outstanding men had not entered the clerical profession after finishing their theological studies; and two of them, Hegel and Schelling, had eventually become professors of philosophy. But the third, the poet Hölderlin—passive and sensitive like Mörike— had gone from one tutorial position to another and had not been able to reconcile the demands of this vocation with those of his poetic imagination. Mörike was to face a similar struggle between his own inclinations and the demands of his profession. He was to break away from it after a few years. But he quickly returned after realizing that his poetic gifts were not those of a writer for magazines.

During his years of preparation for the clergy, Mörike was not a good student either at the preparatory school in Urach or, after the four years there, at the theological seminary, the so-called Stift, in Tübingen. The teachers hardly appreciated his poetic interests. In this respect, his fellow students were much more perceptive, as is shown by the following anecdote told by his life-long friend and admirer, Wilhelm Hartlaub:

When he could be visited again [after he had been ill with scarlet fever], the fellow-students flocked to him in their free hours. Out of curiosity I went along one day. But what happened to me there! He delighted and entertained the swarm around him with a hundred jests; nothing he said was ordinary, but he radiated the most happy sunshine, in which everybody at once felt gay. Then the crowd disappeared as it had come, but I must have sensed what Ludwig Bauer says

of Mörike: that he was Poetry incarnate, meaning by Poetry everything that is good, beautiful, dear, and worthy of love. I have loved
him ever since.[1]

As far as the demands of the school were concerned, it appears
as if Mörike had a gift for protecting his privacy under any circumstances; he developed a certain immunity to the rules,
which sometimes got him into trouble with the school officials.
Often, however, his teachers and tutors must have excused him
as a "dreamer." Perhaps his health also procured him a milder
treatment; he was subject to rheumatic pains and eye trouble,
and in 1823 we hear of an undefined "weakness of the chest."
Today we could venture the hypothesis that he was suffering
from the aftereffects of scarlet fever, but at his time medicine
was not advanced enough to make such a diagnosis. Thus, for
the rest of his life Mörike was blamed again and again for being
a hypochondriac who was imagining pains which had no physical cause. But what appeared as the behavior of a hypochondriac
can also be understood as the peculiar makeup of a poet who
withdrew from everything that might interfere with his moments
of inspiration.

We have an indication of Mörike's psychic activities during
such moments of "absentmindedness" in the following description from the dramatic fragment *Spillner:*[2]

All at once I sense a ringing in my ears, and from that moment on I
feel transported into the strangest circle of thought, as if some magic
pressure were besetting my brain; I am forced to watch the wild mill
which begins to run in my head with ringing and humming; I clearly
feel my condition, but I could not undo the touch of madness that
softly numbed my head more and more. I wondered whether I was
awake or asleep, and for a few moments I believed I had become
clairvoyant; I felt as if my thoughts were tapering off into the finest
points. The fear of ghosts struck me—my state was indeed terrible.
At this moment a quail suddenly began to call in the neighborhood
... all the uneasy thoughts vanished ... my imagination took me into
the open air and verses formed on my lips without my will.[3]

If the poet's mind appears here like an instrument of a higher
power which can inflict terror upon him as well as the bliss of
an inspired moment, such an understanding may have been sug-

gested to Mörike in Tübingen by the sight of the older poet Hölderlin, whose mind was broken by his powerful visions. Hölderlin was not the only one in Tübingen who incited Mörike's thoughts about the poet's relationship to life and society. There was a young poet, Wilhelm Waiblinger, in the "Stift" with Mörike whom he admired for his genius and the ease with which he wrote a novel in the vein of Hölderlin's *Hyperion* during their school years. But Waiblinger's imagination and emotions induced him to lead such a wild life that he almost ruined his health and his reputation. Mörike felt that he could not accompany his friend on this path and tried to set forth his reasons in a letter to Waiblinger: "I would be a hindrance to you and you to me, an obstacle in the course which each of us has to take.... It is an old experience of mine that I cannot share Poetry in the companionship with another person who must spread its restlessness and sufferings instead of being reconciled to it completely."[4]

When Mörike wrote this on April 8, 1825, it was not the first time that he withdrew from a relationship with a person of dynamic and mysterious character. A love far deeper than his friendship with Waiblinger had been suppressed by Mörike in the preceding year. During a vacation in Ludwigsburg at Easter of 1823, he and his friends discovered, in a local restaurant, a strange girl, Maria Meyer, whose mysterious beauty excited their young hearts and minds. The owner of the restaurant had found her unconscious outside the town. He had taken her home and employed her as a waitress. But she combined with her gipsy-like appearance such refined manners and a certain literary knowledge that her young admirers took her for a higher being. She told them that she had a disposition for mystical religious beliefs and had been a follower of Madame Krüdener, a visionary. She had fallen ill, however (her moments of unconsciousness may have been caused by epileptic seizures), and had lost contact with the lady.

Since we have no description of Mörike's feelings for Maria from the poet's own hand (except in his poetry), we must turn to the correspondence between his closest friends: his older sister Luise and his friend Ludwig Bauer. Their letters tell us that the poet had fallen desperately in love with the wandering girl.

She must have meant a self-realization, a personification of his innermost thoughts and ideals, or, as Bauer expressed it: "Eduard brought the figure of his Maria before my eyes. My innermost heart trembled, all the depths of my existence were opened to me. Maria who had given and solved the puzzle of life to him, Maria is also the awakened dream of my soul. Maria herself is poetry."[5] How deeply this experience touched Mörike, we can only sense from his almost complete silence about it after he had asked his friends to destroy his letters when he decided to suppress his feelings.

He had resolved to renounce his love after Maria disappeared from Tübingen as mysteriously as she had come. Reports had reached him that she was in Heidelberg leading the life of a vagabond. And when she came back to Tübingen in 1824 and wanted to see him, Mörike avoided a meeting. So hard was his decision not to see her, and so heavily did his rejection of her weigh on his conscience, that it became a psychic trauma. Many years later he revised the poetry he had written during these moments of anguish so as to express his final dictum: that he had failed Love itself.

When he was just beginning to recover sufficiently to fulfill his obligations in school, he was struck by another blow. His younger brother August, whom he had tenderly loved, died suddenly in August, 1824, a few days after they had heard Mozart's opera *Don Giovanni* together. From then on, the two experiences, the loss of Maria and the death of his brother, along with the impression of Mozart's opera that stirred him so deeply, melted into his *noli me tangere* past, as he called it many years later. In 1827 his sister Luise also died after a long illness, and the theme of death and the transitoriness of all things was forever going to run through the poet's writings, interwoven with expressions of courage or modest resignation and of the gaiety and light that break through the darkness.

In the fall of 1826, Mörike's years of study came to an end. He could hope to settle in a country parish somewhere in Württemberg, where he would divide his time between his duties as a curate and his higher calling: poetry. It was customary that the young clergymen from the "Stift" first served as assistants to established vicars for a few years. But in Mörike's case, this period lasted for eight years, during which he was sent from parish to parish. Although he learned from the experience and enjoyed the stay in various parts of the country, these years were exasperating. Sometimes the climate forced him to ask for a transfer. Or he suffered in a different way when he learned that his cousin Klara, for whom he had nourished a love since childhood, had married another minister who had been his predecessor in one of the places where he worked. And everywhere he felt more and more how little he was qualified for his profession.

Mörike was basically a religious person. But his religion was personal and not always in agreement with the teachings of the theologians. He suppressed his own opinions, which he had formed during his period of theological studies. In his own mind he was very sympathetic to the efforts of his friend, David Friedrich Strauss, who subjected the Bible to historical research.[6] But Mörike's religion rested on feeling more than on thought, an inclination to mystical experiences which sprang from the same source as his poetic inspirations. Yet he could not formulate such feelings in the weekly sermons to a small community of farmers who expected to be chided for their weaknesses, and who otherwise caught up on their missing sleep while the minister's words gently flowed over them. Mörike envied his friends who had procured positions with publishing firms and schools, and by February, 1828, they received his appeals for help: "The most pedantic job at a desk . . . anything but a clergyman!"[7]

He asked the consistory for a long leave to nurse his poor health and took his first refuge with his older brother Karl, an official in the little town of Scheer on the Danube. It was spring, and the river seemed alluring and inviting—a swim would return the vigor of youth to the poet. And did not the beautiful brown eyes of the schoolmaster's daughter, Josephine, hold a similar promise? But there was little time for her; before the leave ran out, Mörike had to find a new position or return to the curacy. He went to Stuttgart and, after several weeks of desperate search, signed a contract with the Stuttgart publishing firm owned by the Frankh brothers. He was to write weekly contributions for the *Damenzeitung.* Happy at this turn of events, he moved into a two-room apartment on November 1, 1828.

But after a month he admitted that he had had his doubts

from the beginning and was sure that he had made a mistake. This was worse than preparing the weekly sermons. He could not write on command. And on December 20 he wrote to a friend: "I realized that I could pursue the plans which fill my whole heart on no other spot in the world more certainly and happily than in the garret of a Württemberg parsonage."[8] But when he arrived at his next office near the Danube, he hardly dared to look at the river and the surrounding forests which reminded him of his short freedom.

In May 1829, he was again transferred, this time to Plattenhardt, where the former vicar, Rau, had just died. His widow and two daughters were still in their old home when Mörike arrived. They were friendly to him, and he became part of the family while the Raus were preparing to move away. After a while, Mörike suddenly realized that the quiet ways of the younger girl, Luise, had made a deep impression on him. A year later he recalled his first sentiments in a letter to her:

Your whole appearance, your quiet, reserved attitude, so often misunderstood, your secret visits to the cemetery, that thoughtful staring glance with which you often sat motionless, not hearing the noisy company around you,—all this gave you an awe-inspiring, mysterious, at times even supernatural appearance in my eyes that was sacred to me and inviolable. For sure—strange as it may sound—I often stood near you, not unlike those creatures who are held by the natural magic power of certain snakes.... Most of the time, however, I felt very calm, very harmless and well in your presence. And I am not sorry because the strange feeling has long disappeared now.[9]

It is interesting to note that he was first attracted to Luise by the feeling of something mysterious about her, no matter how clear and idyllic their relationship became later. They saw each other only on short visits, but Mörike's happiness during their walks in the meadows and forests or their reading and chatting at home is reflected in his many letters. So inspiring was this love, which let him sense mystical relationships between himself, Luise, and nature, that his letters read today as another expression of his genius.

Luise's letters have not been preserved. But in time she must have given indications of being dissatisfied with their situation.

He was still a curate, sent from place to place and unable to support a family. Was he making sufficient efforts to improve his condition? Patiently he tried to show her that it would be wiser to wait for a parish in a climate beneficial to his health, and he sent her accounts of the places for which he had applied. Yet at times he too seemed to despair, feeling depressed and robbed of all inspiration by "the indolence and pedantry of his superiors."[10] And he wondered whether the consistory would hold him responsible for the actions of his older brother, Karl, who had become involved in the revolutionary movement of 1830. Karl had been sentenced to a year's imprisonment in the fortress of Hohenasperg, which had long been a symbol of tyranny for all German liberals. And chance would have it that Mörike had described an imprisonment for political reasons in his novel *Maler Nolten (Nolten the Painter)*, which was just being published. The novel itself may have disturbed his relationship with Luise for another reason. She could not help finding similarities between herself and the heroine. But the girl in the novel tended to be overly sensitive. Was that meant to be a reflection of herself? Mörike could no longer defend himself against Luise's doubts, and thus the engagement of four years came to an end in December 1833. Not long thereafter, in 1834, Mörike became the vicar of Cleversulzbach, a small place in the northern part of Württemberg not far from Heilbronn. He was then almost thirty years old.

During the next nine years, the somewhat spacious vicarage at Cleversulzbach became a home for Mörike, his mother, and his sister Klara. He was well liked by his parishioners, who were mainly farmers. If he suffered from frustration and a nervous condition, he also invented his own therapy. He worked in the garden, continued his drawing, and carved utensils for daily use out of wood. At the same time, he allowed himself to be thoroughly spoiled by his mother and sister. He repaid their love with efforts to entertain them by reading aloud, telling stories, and taking them on trips.

Living in the neighborhood were his old friends Justinus Kerner in Weinsberg, David Friedrich Strauss in Sontheim and, above all, Wilhelm Hartlaub in Wermuthshausen. Because the Hartlaubs lived a day's journey away, the friends depended mainly on letters for communication. These flowed abundantly from Mörike's pen, even at times when other friends had to wait for years for an answer from him. Everyone was included in this friendly correspondence: Mörike's sister and Hartlaub's wife and children, to whom Mörike never tired of sending little poems or gifts. Hartlaub was interested in all his literary plans, even in his small humorous pieces and fairy tales, when other friends reproached Mörike for wasting his talents on such "trifles." Mörike expressed his gratitude for this friendship in a poem "An Wilhelm Hartlaub" (To Wilhelm Hartlaub) in which he pays tribute to Hartlaub's fine piano playing that often delighted him. The poem ends with the idyllic scene of a rural meal.

It is as an idyll that the whole period of Mörike's stay at Cleversulzbach has been judged by his early readers, largely on the basis of another poem, "Der alte Turmhahn" (The Old Weathercock). The poem depicts the ideal life of a country parson through the eyes of a weather cock who has been moved from the church tower to the top of a tile stove in the parson's study. What was a poetical idealization was taken for the poet's real-life situation, although the fact that, unlike the parson in the poem, Mörike had neither wife nor children might have warned the readers against such an oversimplified interpretation. Unlike the friendly, modest parson, Mörike must have felt dissatisfaction at times with his daily life among the farmers. His poetic self was at home in an entirely different world, in the circle of great minds, Goethe and Schiller for example, whose published letters, he felt, expressed many of his own ideas.[11] And when his friend Friedrich Theodor Vischer began to publish esthetic writings, he read them with keen interest.[12]

In the meantime, the old struggle with his poor health and his antipathy to preaching also continued in these outwardly idyllic years. When his mother died, leaving him without the obligation of supporting her, he neglected his duties and left them to curates as often as possible. In November 1842, his superiors gave him the choice of either doing his work without help or going into retirement on a very low pension. Mörike chose retirement; and at thirty-nine he moved with his sister to the spa of Schwäbisch-Hall to take the waters and then at the end of 1844, when the climate there still proved too harsh, to Bad Mergentheim.

Literary historians up to this day have felt that—much as they admire Mörike's work—they had to make apologies for the man who gave up the duties of his professional life so easily. Some of his friends, such as Vischer, shrugged their shoulders and thought him weak; modern critics under the influence of psychology think of him as a psychopath or conjure up the German *Urangst,* that deep-seated fear of "being at the mercy of dark mysterious forces—which drove Mörike to seek security in twilight rooms."[13] These critics contrast Mörike to the psychologically "normal," chiding him for his idiosyncrasies without understanding that these were signs of the sensitivity of a poet whose nerves reacted to the slightest changes in atmosphere, which he so beautifully depicted in his poetry. Had they, instead, established a comparison with other men like him, his eccentricities would have appeared quite mild. It was his instinct as a poet that taught him to seek out the "twilight" which proved a stimulus to his inspiration.[14] He could be loyal to his higher calling only if he gave up preaching, which had caused him so much nervous tension. In previous times, poets had found patrons who freed them from financial worries, Mörike had to be satisfied with a modest pension and the generosity of his friend Hartlaub, who helped him to pay his most pressing debts. It seems tragic, then, that he gained his freedom too late to enjoy it, since his health never improved sufficiently to allow him more than a few hours of productivity for weeks or months at a time.[15]

Although Mörike was now at the end of his ministry, the years in Mergentheim turned out to be a beginning rather than an end. Klara and he had moved into the house of a retired lieutenant colonel, von Speeth, and they soon became close friends of his daughter Margarete, who was nursing her father in his final illness. After his death, Margarete appeared very frail and in need of love and care, a condition which appealed to Mörike's imagination. Soon he was addressing Margarete as "his other sister," giving her the same place in his affection as Klara. She must have moved into a similar position in the little household, since the account book soon showed entries from her hand.

This account book has been published because of the many charming or satirical illustrations Mörike drew in the margins as a running commentary not only on their expenditures for food, clothes, and parties, but also on events which had no connection with their budget. Thus, we know when Gretchen went on a trip or returned, when they had visitors, and so on. The book also tells the touching story of how the monthly pension of 250 florins would never stretch far enough, and how the rare amounts received from publishers had to be used immediately to pay off at least part of the debts. But Mörike always appears just enough above his troubles to treat them with humor.

Mörike's relationship with Margarete became more intimate, and new problems had to be faced. The von Speeths were Catholic. This did not disturb Mörike, who had never been strongly orthodox in his views and, at times, had found the Catholic ritual more attractive than the Protestant service.[16] But his friend Hartlaub protested, and Mörike and Klara were scolded for their intimacy with a Catholic. It speaks for the strength of Mörike's attachment that the Hartlaubs' attitude did not influence him. He resisted their pressure, and they finally weakened. The same was true for Margarete's mother who, at first, did not consider this Protestant middle-class man who subsisted on a small pension a fitting match for her daughter. But she was won over too, and the couple was married on November 25, 1851, after they had known each other for seven years.

The courtship had put an end to the two years' silence of Mörike's poetic genius just after his retirement. The years after 1845 were very fruitful ones for the poet. He wrote a number of masterly poems, often in classical meter, and a longer most delightful poem or short epic "Idylle vom Bodensee" (Idyl from Lake Constance) (1846), portraying the landscape and people he had visited in 1840 on a trip with his brother Louis. During these years, his works also found wider recognition, although many readers preferred the works of other writers with philosophical or political tendencies or exotic settings that were the fashion of the day. The recognition of his delicate art brought Mörike honors and presents from the royal families of Württemberg and Bavaria; it helped to lighten his financial burden when it took the form of stipends from the Tiedge- or Schiller-

Foundations, and it brought him into closer contact with other artists he had long admired. Most valuable for us in this connection is his correspondence with the poet Theodor Storm in the 1850's and the painter Mortiz von Schwind from 1863 to 1871, which affords us an insight into the poet's plans and their sources and execution.

Mörike's marriage had to bring about a change in his professional status. A parson's pension could not feed a growing family, and Mörike had to search for an additional source of income. Just before the wedding, he gave up his lodgings in Mergentheim and accompanied his sister on a trip to Lake Constance, where he hoped to start a small boarding school for girls. The school did not materialize, but he went to Stuttgart and found a position as a lecturer on German literature at a well-known high school for girls, the *Katharinenstift*. Mörike was to remain there for the next fifteen years. It appeared to be the ideal position for him, since his duties were both light and pleasant—he taught only one course in the highest grade—and were stimulating for the poet himself. He prepared his lectures carefully and read widely and thoroughly, annotating, for example, the editions of Goethe's and Schiller's works he had received from the publisher Cotta as partial remuneration for his own works. During these years he further renewed his interest in philosophy, studying the works of Schleiermacher and Schopenhauer.[17] So absorbed was he by his studies that his sister at times could not even arouse his interest in a poetic task such as a poem for a friend whom he was usually happy to oblige.[18]

He did, however, find some time for his own works during these happy years. In 1852, Mörike published one of his most delightful works, "Das Stuttgarter Hutzelmännlein." ('Hutzel' refers to dried pears or apples. The 'little man' of the title is a dwarf-like good spirit of the shoemaker's craft in Stuttgart. In the story he gives the hero, the shoemaker Seppe, a sort of fruitcake which will always grow again if the owner does not swallow the last bite.) This cheerful story of robust Swabian people 500 years ago was followed in 1853 by another fairy tale of completely different character: "The Hand of Jezerte," a delicate tale in "archaic style."[19] In 1856 Mörike then published his masterpiece, "Mozart on the Way to Prague." Friend Hartlaub had urged him to characterize his favorite composer in a short sketch from his life as early as 1847 and called his attention to a biography of Mozart which had just come out. Mörike must have formed his "inner image" of the artist over all these years, carefully avoiding the reading of a more voluminous biography until he had sent his own manuscript to the publisher. In his novella he shows a deep insight into the other artist's character in a few scenes of his own invention. It was the last long work he was able to finish. For twenty years, until his death in 1875, he tried to give new shape to his early novel *Nolten the Painter*, but he had to leave the new version unfinished. It would be wrong, however, to believe that Mörike's poetic power had left him with the completion of the Mozart novella. He continued to write masterful shorter poems, such as "Besuch in der Kartause" (Visit to the Carthusian Monastery) in 1861 or "Erinna an Sappho" (Erinna to Sappho) in 1863, and even cycles of poems like "Bilder aus Bebenhausen" (Pictures from Bebenhausen) in 1863.

Looking once more at his daily life in Stuttgart, we observe a great change in his situation. He was overwhelmed by visitors now and was so swamped by manuscripts from young authors that he had to announce in the paper that he simply could not oblige everyone with his critical opinion. He also took greater interest in public affairs, favoring Bismarck's attempts to unify Germany.[20] Gretchen bore him two daughters, in 1855 and 1857, respectively. He had always loved children and now devoted much of his time to their play, invented games and stories for them, and watched over them during their childhood illnesses. But this happy home life began to show signs of strain as the poet and his wife became older. Gretchen had always been a very sensitive person and took her illnesses just as seriously as the poet did his. Also the situation with Klara, who had looked after her brother for so long, must have been harder and harder on a wife who had an inclination to jealousy. In 1863 Mörike spent some time with Klara and his younger daughter Marie in Bebenhausen in order to escape the noisy life in the city. In 1866 he gave up the position at the Katharinestift, moved to Lorch, where he felt happy among the farmers and craftsmen, and took up pottery as another outlet for his creativity. But keeping two households proved too heavy a financial burden. He returned to Stuttgart, but the deep-seated resentment in the family made life there unbearable for him; thus, he left again with Klara and Marie for a visit with the Hartlaubs. Gretchen interpreted this as his first step toward a separation and returned to Mergentheim where she spent the rest of her life.

Mörike had suffered bitterly from his quarrels with Gretchen and was miserable. His financial situation again became quite desperate; and, in addition, he had the heartbreaking experience of watching his delicate younger daughter become weaker and weaker. (Marie died of tubercluosis one year after the poet's own death.) His own illness caused him constant pain, and his death on June 4, 1875 was not unexpected. On his previous birthday, he had heard mysterious music which no one else noticed, and he said: "That means me. This is my last birthday."[21]

CHAPTER 2

Mörike, the Lyricist

I. *His Place in Literary History*

MÖRIKE is most famous for his lyric poetry. In his poems he attained heights that have hardly been surpassed. His achievement is not only a perfection of form, which of itself might leave the reader impressed but somewhat cold; in Mörike's poems the content gives life and warmth to meter, rhyme, and rhythm. However, a limited number of experiences and themes establish the content of his poetry. Mörike's poetry is not *Gedankenlyrik* (philosophical poetry) like Schiller's. In it thoughts are transformed into feelings and moods. Only occasionally does he conclude a poem with a few lines which sum up the deeper meaning of its content. His poetry is never didactic; it exists for its own sake. But this does not mean that it is hermetic and available only to the initiated; his carefully chosen words appeal to everybody who has an ear for words.

Mörike has often been considered as a particularly Swabian author.[1] Such a classification rests, however, on a very narrow basis, that is, on some of his prose and occasional poetry. He has also been called a romanticist because of his poems of longing and melancholy, his wish for a union with nature, and his predilection for twilight and darkness. On the other hand, he has been claimed as a member of the group of *Biedermeier* poets, since he was interested in apparently unimportant things and often admonished himself to be content with a very modest share in life; indeed, he prayed to God not to overwhelm him with too many joys—or sufferings. (See the poem "Gebet" [Prayer].) While the references to Mörike as a Romantic and *Biedermeier* poet were made by later literary historians, Mörike's friends compared him over and over again with the greatest of German lyricists, Goethe, and considered him closer to the master (who was still alive when Mörike began to write but did not live to see the first edition of Mörike's poems appear in 1838) than any other contemporary.

In our own time, some critics have again placed him near Goethe because of his striving for clarity, form, and mastery of life's problems.[2] They interpret his idyllic poetry and his fairy tales as an expression of superiority over the threatening darkness that appealed to many romanticists. Other critics have recently evaluated Mörike's "flight into the idyllic" as a means of escape. And wherever Mörike gave vent to his pleasure in speaking through various humorous characters, such as Wispel or the Trusty Man, they took these inventions for masks behind which he tried to hide his awareness of danger, chaos, and the futility of all things.[3] It is obvious that these critics were carried away by their eagerness to make Mörike a modern poet. Yet there seems to be no need for distortion to make his response to life relevant to us. There is, indeed, ample proof that he was aware of the tragic and demonic, but, at least in his poetry, he strove to overcome it and display courage and joy in the abundance of earthly beauty and human experience.

In the following discussion of individual works, reference will be made to such terms as "Classicism," "Romanticism," or *Biedermeier* and to the scholarly discussion concerning Mörike. The emphasis, however, will be on analyzing the texts, following the process of poetic imagination, and tracing the interplay of content and form in his work.

II   *The Role of Nature in Mörike's Poetry*

The body of Mörike's poetry is not large. And among his published poems—mainly among the posthumously published ones—quite a few are occasional pieces dedicated to certain persons or special events. A number of poems consist of only a few lines, but they are often the perfect expression of a thought or scene from human life or nature. Frequently a sudden flash seems to strike the poet, and an object or experience stands out from everyday life or quite common surroundings, excites his imagination, joins together with memories, and is transformed as if by magic while it is being put into words, as in the following poem, "Im Park" (In the Park):

Look, the chestnut tree's are still children,
                    they hang here as moist as the
Wing of the butterfly when it has just left its wrap;
But a short rain in a gentle night brings to unfolding
Softly the fanshaped leaves. Quickly they cover the path.
—You may hurry, O heavenly spring, or you may linger,
Always a wonder, you flee past our enraptured eye.[4]

This is not one of Mörike's early poems. (It was written in 1847,[5] while his earliest poetry stems from 1820.) But in spite of its shortness it contains so many of the characteristics of his art that it may serve as an introduction. We only need to focus attention on the first word, and, at once, we find that the poet turned directly to his readers in order to make them share his experience. We will hear this appeal more often as we continue our studies. Reading on in this poem, we quickly sense the rhythm of the classical distich. (A line of six stresses is followed by one in which the sixth beat is incomplete.) The leading image of the poem is that of a young leaf of a chestnut tree, which is compared to other young creatures: children, for whom Mörike had such an affinity, butterflies, the delicate beings which poets often use as symbols of the divine spirit or the human soul or, also, of the frailty of all things. Thus, the comparison with the butterfly and its associations gives us the first hint at the essence of the little poem: the swiftness with which spring passes.

In the third line, motion is introduced into the stationary scene of the hanging leaves: the rain of one night causes them to open. And the open leaves provide a roof over the path, which is lined with chestnut trees. Our view is thus widened from the single leaf to the whole line of trees, and these again stand for spring as a whole.

The very last lines are rather enigmatic. Mörike often puzzles his readers by using a word or a line ambiguously. How strongly did he feel the sadness hidden in the words "flee" and "past" here when he combined them with "wonder"? The next-to-the-last line seems to indicate that spring might stay longer. But the last line obviously means that even then spring would be passing too swiftly. Yet the impact of this statement of transitoriness is softened by the inserted "wonder" and the rich feeling of the word "enraptured" in front of "eye." The reader, therefore, gains an experience of wealth and abundance rather than of melancholy.

One other aspect of the poem "In the Park" is very character-istic of Mörike: in the last two lines he addresses spring itself. This presupposes a feeling of close relationship with nature. We find something similar in a poem written more than four years earlier about "Die schöne Buche" (The Beautiful Beech Tree), where the poet ends his description of a natural phenomenon with a few personal remarks about the solitude surrounding the tree:

Deep in the forest I know of a place that is carefully hidden,
  There I found growing a beech fairer than pictures can show.
Smooth is its stem and pure and proudly alone it is rising.
  None of its neighbors can touch it in its sericeous dress.
Everywhere underneath the range of the stately tree's branches
  Grows the grass in a ring, pleasant and cool for the eye.
Equally far on all sides it surrounds the stem in the center.
  Artless nature itself created this beautiful round.
Delicate bushes at first encircle it like a green wreath.
  Beyond them the tall-stemmed trees keep out the heavenly blue.
Next to the darker wealth of the oaktree, the birch gently swaying
  Offers her maiden hair shyly to gold-giving light.
Only here, where the footpath covered by rocks steeply slants,
  Can I, behind the glade, sense the wide-open field.
—Recently, when I walked lonely, losing my path in the bushes,
  Tempted and led astray, looking at summer's new forms,
Suddenly to my surprise here I was led by a genius,
  Friendly he was, harkening god of the hallowed grove.
What a delight I felt! The sun was just high in its zenith,
  All was still, quiet were even the birds in the leaves,
After a moment's delay, I stepped on the elegant carpet,
  Only quite softly I walked, splendor was meeting my foot.
Then, while I leaned on the stem right under the tree's arching
                                                          branches,
  (It starts its vault not too high) wandered my eyes in the round
Over the shadowy circle to where the sunbeams were flaming
  Forming a dazzling rim equally measured around.
But I stood and I moved not; to the demoniac quiet,
  To the unfathomed peace listened my innermost soul.
When I was closed in with *you* in these sunny and magic surroundings
  Nothing I felt and I thought, *Solitude!,* only you![6]

[*29*]

At first glance, the poem seems to be what we call a *Dinggedicht:* a description of an object in nature (or art) so impersonal that the object appears to reveal its life rather than the poet his thoughts and feelings. This requires a certain degree of self-denial on the part of the poet. And critics have pointed to Mörike's gift for letting the object speak for itself as another instance of his hiding behind masks. But, at least for this poem, such a theory cannot be upheld. Not only is the objective description of the beech tree introduced as a very personal experience in the first two lines; the second part of the poem abounds with references to the poet's own feelings: he was tempted, surprised, delighted, and then he felt "Solitude." If we take "the demoniac quiet" and "the unfathomed peace" of the preceding lines as synonyms for "Solitude," we sense even more than from the former expressions of delight that "Solitude" must not be understood as loneliness in the sense of being without company.[7] Rather, we are touching on a mysterious depth which Mörike was to describe again and again in various terms. To him it was the realm from which he derived his inspiration. It is this moment which he describes in the last lines that made the entire poem possible. We have here another description of the poetic moment. The poet allows us a glance into his sanctuary. He is far from hiding behind the object; and the poem is an *Erlebnisgedicht,* the rendering of a personal experience.

In another poem, also dating from the 1840's "Auf eine Christblume" (On a Christmas Rose), we hear much less about the poet and his personal feelings. But he addresses the flower so tenderly as "daughter of the forest, related to the lily" and describes how he had looked for it and finally found it for the first time in the cemetery, that we sense his adoration of the flower even in the later verses when he calls the flower "child of the moon" and relates its whiteness and scent to the Holy Virgin's bridal gown. He makes no reference to the inception of this poem in the work itself. In this instance, we have to resort to his letters.

In a letter to Hartlaub, dated October 29, 1841, we find a description of the experience which nurtured this poem. Mörike and his sister had, indeed, found a Christmas rose. They had taken it home and placed it in a glass near the window. The next morning it had mysteriously disappeared. This experience was corroborated by information from an almanac, which strengthened the poet's impression that the Christmas rose had mystical qualities. In the letter he mentions that he hopes to translate his experience into poetry. Almost a month later, on November 26, 1841, he sent Hartlaub a poem with the title "The Christmas Rose" and offered to insert yet another stanza between the next to last one, with its references to Christ's suffering and to Christmas time, and the very last one, in which an elf stands touched by the mystical glory of the flower. A few days later, on December 3/4, 1841, however, he sent another poem of two stanzas with the title "On a Christmas Rose." And when the poems were printed in the following year, they appeared as two individual pieces. Only in 1844 did he join them in a new manuscript under the common title "On a Christmas Rose."[8]

This information about the origin of the poem "On a Christmas Rose" is important for us because it is an indication of a conscious effort on the poet's part. Mörike rarely admitted that he had to struggle with the material for his poetry. He liked to create the impression that his verses formed "under his hands by themselves" (see the poem "Am Walde" [At the Forest]). This image of the poet who is writing by inspiration alone must be corrected, however, on the basis of earlier and later versions of some of his works. The changes his poems underwent are a clear indication of Mörike's conscious efforts which were guided by his knowledge of artistic forms and their effect on the reader.[9]

A comparison of the poem "On a Christmas Rose" with other poems by Mörike tells us yet another secret about his creative process: he often shifted individual motifs from one poem to another. Thus the combination of moonlight and lilies had appeared much earlier in the second poem of the Peregrina cycle (1824), and the idea of the butterfly that carries the sacred spirit of the Bible to a lily, where in turn "the best of all girls" will sense it, was used in the poem "Im Weinberg" (In the Vineyard) (1838). Now, in the second part of the poem "On a Christmas Rose," it is only the delicate spirit of the butterfly that could possibly circle the flower in wintertime unseen by the poet. The artistic use of this motif gives perfect expression to the "mystical" that Mörike sensed in the flower.[10]

In his letter to Hartlaub, Mörike also mentions that the flower engendered in him a feeling of longing. But he did not express this feeling in the poem as he had done in his earlier poetry. This is perhaps one of the most obvious differences between the relatively objective descriptions of things and experiences of his mature years and the subjective poetry of his youth.

We have started our discussion with a few poems from Mörike's middle years in order to furnish some examples of what could be called his objective poetry. To understand and appreciate these we do not need to know anything about the poet, his age, or the philosophy of his period. Form and images of "In the Park" or "The Beautiful Beech Tree," for example, are common property of Western culture and could be favorably compared to many ancient poems as well as the works of modern authors in other countries who are striving for the objectivity of classicism. We shall see more examples of such poetry by Mörike in the chapters that are not concerned with nature. In our present discussion of his poems on nature, however, we must look at his earlier works.

In the last analysis, such a division into earlier and later periods is artificial. Most likely, the tendency toward "objective" and "subjective" poetry was at all times present in the poet's character. This can be substantiated on the basis of Mörike's letter of May 4, 1829, in which he indicates the wish to rid himself of all his subjective material after having distilled a general and pleasantly mixed truth from it. In the same letter he contrasts his own subjectivity with the objective discussion of literary questions in the correspondence between Goethe and Schiller.[11] This was the level he hoped to attain eventually after a period of writing about feelings and problems which concerned him personally. The poem "An eine Äolsharfe" (To an Äolian Harp), from 1837, may be read as a result of this ambiguous situation. The poem at first seems to concentrate on the object, the harp, which is played by the winds rather than by human touch. But then the description of this phenomenon is fused with personal feelings, and the sounds of the harp become the mode of expressing these feelings.

To an Äolian Harp

Leaning against the ivy-clad wall
Of this ancient terrace
You, who sounds
So mysterious when touched by an air-borne muse
Begin
Begin again
Your melodic lament!

You, winds, come here from afar
Alas, from the freshly greening
Hill of the boy
Whom I loved
And gliding over the flowers of spring on your way
Saturated with pleasant scent
How sweet is your touch for this heart!
You whisper gently through the strings
Attracted by sweet-sounding sadness
Growing with the pulse of my longing
And calming down again.

But suddenly
As the wind blows more strongly
A lovely cry of the harp
Repeats to my sweet alarm
The sudden move of my soul
And here—the full-blooming rose strews when it's shaken
All its petals down at my feet.[12]

At first glance, the poem appears to be written in free verse. But when it is read carefully, the meter of ancient odes can be sensed as underlying Mörike's changing rhythm in certain lines.[13] The motto Mörike inserts between the title and the first stanza is also a verse from an ode by Horace. It speaks of melodies of mourning over the death of a beloved, and of the longing that does not stop when night comes or goes. Thus, not only the form but also the content of Mörike's poem was suggested by the ancient motto. He simply seems to elaborate on his theme when he addresses the musical instrument, the harp that is played by the wind. But in the next stanza we cannot help but feel his personal involvement when he speaks of the boy whom he loved— it is generally accepted that he was thinking of his brother August, who died very early. Yet the sadness of the experience is transformed into beauty. The winds touch not only the grave but also the flowers of spring. The music reflects the resulting mood of the poet in "sweet-sounding sadness." This repetition, at the end of the second stanza, of the mood described by the words "melodic lament" in the first seems to establish such a mixture of longing and resignation (calming down) as final. But the poem does not really end here. The third stanza brings a sudden change. The wind blows more strongly, the soul is suddenly stirred, and nature gives more to the poet than consolation: it reminds him of the full beauty of the present when the rose strews its petals down at his feet.

This is one possible interpretation of the concluding lines, but not the only one. Since it is not the rose as a whole that falls at the poet's feet, the image may also symbolize the early death of the youth in his bloom. Knowing Mörike's great sensitivity for the language, we must presume that he was aware of both readings. That he did not want to suggest the second version only is clear from the entire final stanza with its "lovely cry of the harp" and the "sweet alarm." More than the words, the sounds in the final lines impart the feeling of wealth and fulfillment.

The whole poem is very melodious. Even if we could not understand the words, the rhythm would indicate the changes from calm to longing and to eager expectation. The consonants also contribute to this effect: there is much alliteration in the German, as in "Wie der Wind heftiger herstößt" or "Wohllautende Wehmut" (my emphasis). Such verses, where language speaks so directly to the listener that he does not have to think about the content first, can be compared to the *poésie pure* of the French Symbolists.[14]

In many respects, the following poem, "Frühling" (In Spring) is very similar to the poem "To an Äolian Harp." Yet it was written nine years earlier, in 1828. It has a similar metric pattern, and it also lives from the sound of the words as much as their meaning. It reveals mixed sentiments, "partly joy and partly grief," and is also a poem of longing. The earlier poem differs from the one above by not turning to the present moment at the end. Instead, the poet delves deep into the heart for "old days which you cannot retrieve!"

[*34*]

In Spring

On the vernal hill of flowers I lie here:
The cloud's my wing and heaven so near,
A bird is bidding me on his way.
O tell me, Love, my only guide,
Where you're at home, there I abide!
But you and the wind have no place to stay.

The sunflower waits—but my heart even more,
It is yearning
And burning
To love and adore.
Spring, what is your intent?
Will you make me content?

The cloud I see wander and the stream,
I feel the sunshine's golden beam
Down in my blood very deep;
My eyes are so overwhelmed by this glee,
They act as if falling asleep,
Yet I can still hear the sound of the bee.
My mind is wandering astray,
I yearn, but for what I could not say:
'tis partly joy and partly grief;
Tell me, my heart, what to believe
What is it that you remember
In the faint light of green branches' amber?
Old days which you cannot retrieve!

This is the poem of yearning. Nature is filled with longing;
the winds and the birds feel it, and also the human heart. Its
hope is so vague as to be indescribable. But in the end the poet
startles us: when he speaks of hope, instead of thinking of the
future, he turns back to the past. Longing for the past, however,
is considered a romantic quality. We find it often in the poems
of the young Mörike. This early poetry is romantic also in its
tendency to melancholy, a predilection for darkness or twilight,
the experience of the short duration of love. No doubt, Mörike's
early responses to life resembled those of the romanticists in
many ways.

But Mörike did not imitate them, as is shown by the poem
"Mein Fluss" (My River) which appears so romantic when it

depicts the poet's wish to unite with the water, and yet is so different from a romantic poem with its recognition that nature does
not accept human love. Twice the poet offers himself to the
water. The first time, his chest and cheeks are given to the
caressing waves as the poet wades into the river. Then the water
releases him, but it seems to the poet that the river wants to reveal an old story, a fairy tale it has carried for a long time. The
poet attends carefully with all his senses, but he can only guess
that the reflection of the sky is the river's soul. This soul is as
deep as love. And again the poet attempts a union with nature,
this time offering his life to its dangers in Dionysian ecstasy. In
vain, the river rejects him cajolingly and returns to its mother
source alone.

This poem is one of many utterances in which Mörike indicates his concern about the relationship between man and nature
and a possible union of the two. In this connection he shows
more skepticism than the Romanticists and often indicates a certain bitterness at nature's indifference toward man's happiness
and suffering.

The secrets of nature are used thematically in the poem "Besuch in Urach" (Visit in Urach), written in 1827 on the occasion
of a visit to the town where Mörike had spent four years in the
preparatory school. "Visit in Urach" is often compared with
Goethe's poem "Ilmenau." In that poem, Goethe interpolated
events of two different periods of his life. He blended his early
years in Weimar with the moment at which he wrote the poem
seven years later. Mörike's poem is also filled with memories
of the past and experiences of the moment. It is skilfully composed of twelve stanzas in *ottava rima*. Almost every line brings
out some peculiarities of the poet. Thus, in the opening lines he
declares that the whole visit occurred as in a dream; and we are,
of course, reminded of the importance of dreams in romantic
poetry. Mörike himself developed a theory of the interrelationship of the different mental states: that of being awake and that
of his dream life.[15] At the end of the first stanza of "Visit in
Urach," he continues his description of the mixed state of mind
that besets the poetic "I" in the poem: "Truth itself becomes
fiction here, my own image a strange and pleasing sight!" (Mörike
writes *"hold Gesichte,"* and both words can be translated in vari-

ous ways: *hold* means also lovely and graceful. It is one of the poet's favorite words, which he laboriously tried to replace in later editions of his works.[16] *Gesichte* could be "second sight" or vision, or simply countenance.) The central lines tell us what confuses him so: it is the past that seems to look at him out of a thousand green mirrors. And filled with melancholy, grief, and joy, he sinks into it more deeply, as the poem continues. But he does not want to surrender to these feelings. "I must go" (*Hinweg!*) he says to himself, leaving the past and returning to the present. And now he goes through the same experience as in "My River":

> O here it is where nature tears the veil!
> For once it breaks its superhuman silence;
> And talking loudly to itself its spirit
> Wants to reveal its secrets while it listens.[17]

These lines are somewhat atypical in that their overabundance of thought is not really transformed into a poetic image. The poet then offers to unite with the water—this time it must have been the beautiful waterfall near Urach that inspired these lines— but he is not accepted by nature. And again he pulls himself away: "I must go"—this time from the overwhelming beauty of nature—and turns to a modest corner where in his youth a hut and a bench used to offer a cozy hiding place. There follow three extraordinarily beautiful lines, in which the abstract idea of remembrance has truly become poetry:

> Remembrance with a smile hands me the magic cups
> Which are embittered and so sweetened as to lull me;
> And eagerly I drink enraptured tortures.

In the German, the rhyme and sound of these lines persuade the reader that the magic potion is irresistible:

> Erinnrung reicht mit Lächeln die verbittert
> Bis zur Betäubung süßen Zauberschalen;
> So trink ich gierig die entzückten Qualen.

In the following stanzas, the poet suffers the torture of a detailed recollection of earlier days of love and happiness. It is so overwhelming that he finally throws himself down with the words:

[37]

"Pleasure is gone! May everything run its course!" But this is not the conclusion of the poem. He is suddenly aroused by the distant noise of a thunderstorm. This extreme action in nature always had a strong effect on Mörike.[18] He feels at once rejuvenated and can now leave the valley of his youth with the conviction that the thought of it will give him strength forever.

"Visit in Urach" is one of the poems in which Mörike overcame the temptation to look back into the past and to be caught in melancholy which would make him unable to live in the present. The most wonderful poem of this kind is "An einem Wintermorgen, vor Sonnenaufgang" (On a Winter Morning, before Sunrise.)

On a Winter Morning, before Sunrise

O time as light as down when night expires!
Which world is it you stir in me so new?
What is it that at once I now in you
Feel all aglow with living's soft desires?

My soul is lucid now, like crystal clear,
That never did a false ray penetrate;
My mind now seems to float, then may at rest appear,
As if for magic powers open laid,
Which from blue atmosphere's transparent ring
A magic word at last will to my senses bring.

My eyes are open, yet I mean to reel;
I keep them closed, that not the dream may flee.
Do I look down in fairies' revery?
Who did invite the motley crew, I feel,
Of images and thoughts to my heart's shrine,
Like sparkling gold-fish which in garden-ponds we see?

This sound that to the shepherd's flute belongs,
Was heard around the manger long ago,
Now vine-clad youths sing me their joyful songs;
Who could it be that brought these peaceful throngs
Into my walls that were so filled with woe?

And what a feeling of enraptured power!
For new adventures I am in the mood!
When with the early vigor of this day imbued,
I sense for any enterprise the hour.

[38]

My soul flies up as far as heav'n expands,
And genius exalts in me! But say
Why is it now that sorrow wets my glance?
Is it lost happiness that ties my hands?
Is it a future one my heart does pray?
—Move on, my mind! Inaction you must banish:
It's just a moment, everything will vanish!

There see! At the horizon rises high the curtain now!
The day is dreaming, and the night must bow;
The crimson lip that firmly closed lay,
Exhales half opened lovely breath so light:
At once the eye now sparks, and like a god, the day
Begins by leaps and bounds its royal flight![19]

Following the suggestion of Mörike's friend Hermann Kurz, this poem is found at the beginning of all collections of Mörike's poetry. No other poem seems as well suited to introduce the poet's works as this one, which tells so much about the creative moments of its author. What is described as a moment of madly confused impressions in the fragment *Spillner* here appears as a moment of ecstasy. The soul is compared to the crystal untouched by light; it is purified of all unhappy memories it may have had; the heart is filled with images ready to become poetry, and the mind feels strength to work again. No other poem gives such beautiful expression to the poet's most cherished experience. Lately, "On a Winter Morning, before Sunrise" has also been treated as the poem that best illustrates Mörike's position in German intellectual history. In 1939 the Swiss literary historian Emil Staiger drew a sharp line between Goethe and the Romantic poet Brentano on the basis of their experience of time.[20] To Goethe he ascribed the ability of experiencing eternity within the present moment, of abstracting the idea from a variety of given objects, while he felt that Brentano lacked circumspection and could only experience one impression after another, without connecting them mentally. Brentano, in this view, did not have the assurance of something lasting in the flow of time. In 1947 Staiger applied this method of interpreting a poet's work to Mörike's poem "Das verlassene Mägdlein" (The Forsaken Girl).[21] He decided that Mörike could not live fully in the present either but would at once look at an experience as if it were already past. According to Staiger, many of Mörike's poems were fed by remembrances of the past. This view of Mörike was further accentuated by Werner Kohlschmidt, who included the poem "On a Winter-Morning, before Sunrise" in his discussion.[22] He based his argument on the lines:

> But say
> Why is it now that sorrow wets my glance?
> Is it lost happiness that ties my hands?
> Is it a future one my heart does pray?
> —Move on, my mind! Inaction you must banish:
> It's just a moment, everything will vanish!

Here the poet seems to lose all the impetus he had gained in the poem up to this point, because his mind wanders into the past and future. But in making these lines representative for Mörike, Kohlschmidt completely overlooks the message of the final stanza.

The meaning of the last stanza was emphasized in an interpretation of the whole poem by Adolf Beck.[23] Beck also sees the importance of the phase marking the interruption of the moment of exaltation, but for him it is most significant that Mörike tries to overcome this phase. He stresses the lines in which the poet admonishes himself to move on and then points to the last stanza, with the wonderful image of the sunrise, to prove that Mörike was able to overcome moments of melancholy and inertia. In summing up his observations, Beck writes: "A mind striving up into daylight, a soul absorbed by the night: that is Mörike."[24] This feeling has since been shared by other scholars.[25]

Beck also suggests a definite relationship of the poem with Mörike's personal situation at the time of its inception. The poem was written in 1825 and might well symbolize Mörike's recovery from the deep shock which the separation from Maria Meyer and the death of his brother August had inflicted upon him during the previous year. This interpretation is supported by a few lines from the first version in which the poet asked himself: "Is it a god who gave this feeling of strength to you and this sick blood?" thus admitting that he was not only greeting a new morning but also a recovery from a period of suffering. There is a similarity to Goethe's Faust viewing the sign of the macrocosm, which allows Beck to establish a close relationship between the two poets.[26]

A further confirmation of the deeper meaning of the poem "On a Winter-Morning" can be found in another poem, which was written half a year earlier, "Im Freien" (In the Open Air).[27] There the poet asked: "Am I dead for you/immortal spirit of nature?/Was the soft pain/of that unfortunate love/able to estrange you from me for ever?/And thus must I now despair/because I gave my blood/for a shadow?" The poet then turns to asking the winds, heaven, and thunder to stir him "So that it would rouse me/from the unpleasant/feeble death!/Just so that I feel: I live." He now imagines what would happen if his wish were granted: he would see God's admonishing spectacle (the thunderstorm) from a quiet corner and—*while brooding* (my italics)—he would draw strength for his own activity. We know that this wish was granted later; namely, at the time which is reflected in the "Winter-Morning." The earlier poem, however, was definitely a premonition of the recovery. It gives us the cause of the sickness—the unhappy love—as well as the remedy —the spectacle in nature. And still more interesting, it even foresees that the moment of recovery would not be entirely free of brooding.

Mörike had not considered "In the Open Air" worth publishing. We find it in Maync's edition among the poetry that appeared posthumously. It is followed by another poem that represents one of several attempts by Mörike to find the best form for an inspiration that had presented him with the imagery for his experience of night. The unpublished poem bears the title "Nachts" (At Night). Its first half describes the workings of nature before dawn. These lines must have satisfied the poet because he took them over into his shadow-play, "Der letzte König von Orplid" (The Last King of Orplid), which he inserted in the novel *Nolten the Painter*. Of the second part of "At Night" only a few lines were taken over. And they underwent such a change as to indicate a very different attitude of the speaker. In the shadow-play, the king likens his own condition to that of nature, saying that he feels a similar contrast of abundance and privation in his own heart. The situation was quite different in "At Night." There was no privation in nature but powerful fermentation, order, and calm. Only the human observer was troubled by the contrast between the plenty of the surrounding nature and the want in his own heart, which constantly wavers between exuberance and resignation. So overwhelmed is the speaker of this poem by the powerful impressions nature makes on him that he tells his heart: "If you cannot stand up to the divine quiet of beauty,/then bow to it! there is no chance to flee."

This personal reaction to the beauty of night is completely omitted in the other verses which express the poet's fascination with this natural phenomenon. A few such lines followed the hallucinations of the student, Spillner, in the fragment bearing that name. He had experienced a moment in which a number of weird visions seemed to beset his mind. The first sounds from a quail had freed him; he began to watch nature outside of his window, and verses formed on his lips. These verses from the *Spillner* fragment also appear, with a few changes, in the shadow play "The Last King of Orplid," where they are framed by the parts of the poem "At Night" and have been expanded. In all, there are thirty-eight lines, with imagery representing the workings of nature at night. They are divided among two characters of the play, the king and the fairy Thereile. Mörike retained these divisions when he published the central lines independently under the title "Gesang zu zweien in der Nacht" (Song of Two at Night), again omitting the lines of "At Night." The results of his changes are apparent in the following poem:[28]

SHE: How sweet the night-wind over the meadow glides
And tinkling now through the young coppice strides!
When still the insolent day is dumb,
One hears the earthly powers' whispering throngs
Which heavenwards into the tender songs
Of purely tuned breezes hum.

HE: And the most lovely voices meet my ears,
Lustfully carried hither by the genial wind,
While stripes of light at morn's arrival hint
And heaven itself to me afloat appears.

SHE: The air oft quivers like a woof,
More lucid and more luminous to blow;
And in between one hears soft music go
From blessed fays, who under heaven's roof

> At blue spheres' ring,
> Untiring while they sing,
> Twirl silver bobbins to and fro.

HE: O lovely night, you walk with steps so light
On velvet black, green only in the day,
And airy whizzing sounds attend the way
Your foot must take in your most gentle stride,
When hour by hour you measure
And in unbounded pleasure
Forget yourself. Creation's soul joins your delight![29]

If we had not known it already, this poem would tell us that Mörike must have been very sensitive to music. The poem is mainly a rendering of the sounds a very fine ear might hear at night when we cannot depend on our vision. How delicate must have been the nerves of a man who could hear the ringing of the spheres! And the same lines show us something else: Mörike possessed the gift for creating figures, like the fays here, which resembled those of ancient mythology and personified natural phenomena.

This is even more apparent in the poem "Um Mitternacht" (At Midnight) of 1827. In this poem, Night is seen as a figure leaning against the edge of the mountains, watching the scales of time. At midnight the scales appear at rest while they are in balance. But contrasting the majestic calm of this image, which the poet describes with the equally slow measures of iambic meter, we hear the eagerly trickling springs sing to the mother, Night, in dactylic verses, of the day that has passed. Night does not want to listen to their singing and would prefer the sounds of heaven that keep the hasty hours in balance; yet always the springs have the last word and sing of the day. This poem is, therefore, another indication of Mörike's concern with time and his awareness of the transitoriness of all things. But again we have to trust the total impression of the poem, which is one of calm and contrasting gaiety, and admire the artist who could render his experience of time in so objective a manner rather than thinking of the possible despair over the flow of time he may have had to overcome first. The poet who created this mythical figure of Night showed, by this very act, that he had mastered the problem of Time.

[43]

III *Mörike's Myths and His Folk Poetry*

Normally, myths are tales from the early times of a people or of mankind and are concerned with the origins of religious customs, the character of gods, other supernatural beings, or with natural phenomena. Whether they were created rationally by superior minds who wanted to make certain ideas understood by the common people, whether the people as a whole simply believed in these personifications, or whether we should look for help from psychoanalysis for an explanation of their origins has not been decided. In any case, their purpose must have been a serious one, more serious than that of folk tales, which were often told just to amuse. And the ancient myths have been taken very seriously by writers throughout the ages. Their personages and situations have been used over and over again in modern works. Seldom, however, has a modern writer added to the store of mythological figures and tales. Mörike did just that. He personifies the elements and invents new situations in which these personages would be involved; in one case he invents a new place, "Orplid," with its particular people, gods, early tales, and history.

Figures from the land "Orplid" play an independent role in his poetry also. These figures can be fully appreciated only when the whole interrelationship of their existence in the real world of a novel like *Nolten the Painter,* in the phantasmagoric "Orplid" within the novel, and in Mörike's personal life is understood. We will meet with the figure of "the Trusty Man," for example, in the phantasmagoria as well as in an independent poem, and also in the letters of Mörike's friends, who remember an evening in Mörike's house when "the Trusty Man" was acted out by the poet. The same is true of another figure, Wispel, who appears in the phantasmagoria and plays a role in the novel *Nolten.* Wispel is not a mythological but a purely comical figure, a caricature of human characteristics which Mörike disliked. He is extremely self-confident, always appears on the scene (in different disguises) as the one who knows best, speaks in a highly stilted language with many foreign words, but is actually weak and nervous.

"The Trusty Man," however, may at times appear comical, but has much greater depth. He is drawn with the good-natured humor which he himself displays. At first glance, he seems to be a simple-minded, awkward giant who tricks the farmers but does not really harm them; yet when he is reminded of his birth—which took place soon after the Deluge—and is asked for an account of his memories from those early times, he is seized by a feeling of responsibility, which is at once comical and dignified.

The poem about this "Trusty Man," which Mörike wrote in 1837–38,[30] after the figure had played a role in the circle of his friends since 1824, is one of Mörike's masterpieces. In classical hexameter he relates the adventures of his hero. First we hear of his life among the farmers, which consists of doing nothing or of playing such pranks as breaking all the signposts. But one day sudden light fills his cave, as Lolegrin, the son of the goddess Weyla, the protectress of "Orplid," arrives. He was the entertainer of the gods and hoped to provide some extra fun for his audience by setting the "Trusty Man" to work on the task of writing down his memoirs and his view of the world and its origins, and of transmitting it to the ancient heroes and wise men in the realm of the dead. Such knowledge, he says, has been given to the "Trusty Man" by the gods while he was still enclosed in a rock. The rock was his mother, a gigantic toad, who had been transformed soon after his father, a satyr, had wed her. It was a shame that he seemed to have forgotten it all and to have lowered himself to such a disgraceful condition. He had better change soon or the gods would show him their dissatisfaction. That helped.

After Lolegrin left, "the Trusty Man" tried "to let his mind work its way backwards into the mass of many thousands of years." No order was there, no way to relate things—so he had the brilliant idea of making the book first in which to write his account. And now follows a delightful tale of pure humor: the hero is so huge that he needs the doors of the farmers' barns for the pages of his book. He binds them together, and while he is busy at that "the spirit grows in him." He begins to write and writes for a day and a half until the book is filled and he can make the full-stop as large as a child's head. And now he marches down to the place of the shadows deep in the earth, secretly guided by Lolegrin. And he reads about the origin of the earth. (The account he gives is similar to that given by

Plato and in Goethe's *Satyros*.) He feels the importance of his task and does not show his irritation when the devil, who has also sneaked in, begins to play tricks on him. Suddenly, however, he reaches back, seizes the devil's tail, and pulls it off. To the admiring glances of his audience, he puts the tail in the book as a marker and utters a prophecy: "Three times the Trusty Man will hurt the devil before the end of all things comes, for the tail grows again, but each time a little bit shorter; and each time the devil will lose strength, until he will be old and despised and the earth will celebrate and the Trusty Man will become the companion of the gods."

Mörike himself was not as ambitious as "the Trusty Man"; he did not try to explain the origin of the world. But he created a new island in his imagination, the island "Orplid," with its own relationship to the gods and a goddess who favored it in particular. At first, the thought of "Orplid" must have been a pastime for him and his friend Bauer, who later dated the inception of the idea around July 25, 1825. The friends had often withdrawn from school to a lonely room over a well, where they read Homer, Shakespeare, and Goethe—now they kept busy inventing new characters for their island and its involved history. It was to be a place without sickness or hunger, and obviously its inhabitants must have been of an idealistic nature, for as soon as they became too self-certain and refined, they were dropped from the gods' favor. They died, and the island was barren of human beings for almost a thousand years. Almost barren, that is, for Weyla had chosen the finest man, King Ulmon, for a special fate: he was to live on for a thousand years; then the sacred book, which she had hidden, would be found again and one would learn from it that Ulmon could find rest if a child shot an arrow into a black willow tree. To make the fulfillment of this prophecy possible, the island became the refuge of shipwrecked people about seventy years before the appointed time. Among the second generation, there is a man who meets Ulmon and wants to help him. The rascal Wispel and his friend have found a mysterious book, which Ulmon's friend buys from them, and soon Weyla's terms are fulfilled and Ulmon can die and rise to the realm of the gods. This is only the roughest skeleton of the story as Mörike made it available to his readers years after the inception as an inserted shadow play in his *Nolten the Painter*.

The play comprises a number of different scenes. Those with Wispel and his friend remind us of Shakespeare's scenes with rogues. Mörike deliberately coarsened the language to fit the characters. Besides the rogues, there are the normal citizens, who try to overlook the mysterious aspects of life. On still another level we have Ulmon and the man who helps him. They are dignified; yet Ulmon speaks rather diffusely because his memory has suffered over the years. This is his greatest torment; and when he is alone, we see him torture his mind, chide his fate, and suffer from Time. Only in the end does Time lose this character of being man's torture and is transformed into Eternity for Ulmon. Some of the utterances of the suffering king seem to us like premonitions of a more recent concern with Time, be it in the novels of Proust or in the philosophy of existentialism. Also the problem of ennui, of the inability to find a captivating pastime which lets us forget the duration of time, is touched upon. It was yet to torment many of the poets of the nineteenth century. This puts the entire phantasmagoria into a much more serious light. If we take Ulmon as a personification of Mörike's problems, the poet becomes very modern indeed and greatly differs from an ideal country parson leading an idyllic existence. Again Mörike appears to be rather ambiguous, for truly we do not want to discredit his friends entirely, who understood the whole phantasy as a charming and fascinating play of the imagination. It is, by the way, in the phantasmagoria, the shadow play, that we find the "Song of Two During the Night" as part of a scene which quite naturally crystallizes into pure poetry, a reason for discussing the poem along with Mörike's lyrical works. This shows the overwhelming power of the lyrical inclination in the poet, who for a long time tried in vain to create a major dramatic work and finally abandoned this idea. In 1831, "Orplid" and its myth once more gave rise to a few beautiful lines which are widely known in Hugo Wolf's musical setting: "Gesang Weylas" (Weyla's Song).

In Greek mythology, the times of day were also associated with divine figures: dawn with Aurora, night with Hesperus, the coming of the sun with Apollo. In one of his earliest poems, Mörike gave his own allegory for day and night. The setting of the poem is oriental: Night is represented by a slender, beautiful Moorish youth. By playing his harp, he hopes to find his sweetheart; but when she actually appears, he withdraws. She senses that he has been there, yet she will never meet him. This poem is rather conventional. Poets of the Baroque or anacreontic poets might have invented such playful allegory.

We find Mörike going beyond the conventional when he competes with a Romantic such as Brentano in inventing fairy tales, or with Goethe in poetry dealing with the demonic powers of water, wind, and fire. In the novel *Nolten the Painter* he inserted another character who does not belong to the novel proper: Young Volker, the hero of a saga and legend Mörike invented. Volker seems to be a favorite of the gods, the gayest of all rogues. He is a robber but one who is guided by a feeling for justice—he robs only the spendthrift and the infamous. The story becomes a legend the moment he kills a white deer and all at once regrets his un-Christian way of life, dismisses his band of young followers, and goes on a pilgrimage. Before this change, he had also been a minstrel who sang and accompanied himself on his violin. One of his songs described his descent from a union of the wind with a beautiful, audacious woman.

The winds also play a role in connection with Agnes, Nolten's fiancée, who in her distress asks the winds about the nature of love. The answer is evasive and general: "Love is like the wind, quick and lively, it never rests, it is eternal—but not always persistent."

The demonic character of this element is personified in "Die schlimme Greth und der Königssohn" (The Evil Margaret.)[31] In forty-one stanzas of four lines each we hear the tale of the fugitive prince and the girl whom he takes for a miller's daughter. At first she treats him royally to food and drink. They live together, although she warns him that she has to remain a maiden. One day he comes home from hunting with a troubled face, and she asks him point-blank whether he had heard people call her a witch. Because he is now afraid of her, he answers ambiguously, saying that he indeed felt that she had bewitched him, so much so that he thinks of making her his queen as soon as he has won a kingdom. She understands that he wants to leave her and announces that he will first have to see an example of her power. With two wooden spoons she goes to the attic and there winds the fog around the spoons. Out of the fog she calls ghosts whom she orders to wrap up the prince and take him onto the rocks on the seashore. Once more they have a tête-à-tête there. But suddenly her black curls stand up, she presses him against her breast till he suffocates, and then she throws him into the sea.

Certainly the wooden spoons are humorous fairy-tale tools. The undertone of the rapidly moving poem is, however, not humorous at all. It imparts to us the same fear of the luring fateful power of the elements as Goethe's ballads of "Der Fischer" (The Fisherman) and "Der Erlkönig" (King of the Elves). In the "King of the Elves" the fog makes the old willow trees look gruesome and alive, while in Mörike's poem the fog emits the demonic helpers of the wind. In Goethe's "Fisherman," the luring fascination of the water invites the fisherman to his doom, and the same motif underlies a series of Mörike's poems, the "Schiffer- und Nixenmärchen" (Fairy Tales of the Boatsman and the Nixies).

The first of the four poems deals with the magician Drakone and the princess Liligi, whom he instructs about things of the Earth and Heaven, the elements and the stars. Again and again she interrupts and asks him to relate her favorite fairy tales instead: the stories of the "Vom Sieben-Nixen-Chor" (Choir of the Seven Nixies) who cause the boats to sink and invite the drowning prince to their chamber and release him later with seven red wounds. Three times Drakone tells these stories in a hypnotic manner, and the third time the princess falls asleep. He can now take her along and make her a member of the Choir of the Seven Nixies. Poems III and IV also result in the death of those who trust the benevolence of water. In IV the magician's daughter lets the boatsmen forget about the dangers of the waters—she is a relative of Heine's "Lorelei." The waterman's daughter in II acts differently; but she makes her gift to the fisherman's daughter because the girl is going to marry a hunter who will leave the fish alone.

Thus, the elements of nature which Mörike personifies do not always bring death, but they are unreliable; sometimes they only make fun of the mortals who encounter them. If we relate this to Mörike's more direct representations of nature, we are reminded of his recognition that there exists no close tie between man and nature, that nature remains enigmatic, that it incites man's love but does not reciprocate it, and that it might even accept man's death. The underlying fear in the poems just discussed is generally related to the fear of primitive people. Mörike's closeness to their mythical understanding and their manner of expression is usually praised but with the implication that it was also a sign of his backwardness, of an immature reaction toward the power of elements.

Mörike's friends were convinced that the first idea for the masterful poem "Der Feuerreiter" (The Fire-Rider) was born when Mörike observed the mad poet Hölderlin as he wandered back and forth behind the windows of his room, his head covered with a red nightcap. The image of a figure walking up and down behind a window occurs at the beginning of the poem. Then the fire bell sounds from behind the mountain with the call: "There is fire in the mill," and the fire rider is suddenly seen on his skinny horse riding through the gate to the fire. In the first version, of 1824, the poem continued with the statement that the mill burned down in less than an hour and that nobody saw the rider after that. But a human skeleton was found later, seated on the skeleton of the horse leaning against the basement wall. At a touch it turned to ashes. When he revised the poem, in 1841, Mörike added a Christian touch by describing the fire rider's end as a punishment for having used the cross for magic purposes. According to R. Ibel, the poem thereby lost its Dionysian character. Ibel felt that originally the death of the fire rider had been a self-sacrifice.[32] For the rider does, indeed, not represent the fire itself, but rather acts as its opponent. The construction, the rhythm, and the wording are, however, so dense that the reader is hardly aware of the distinction between the fire rider and the fire. He receives, at least upon the first reading, one unified impression of the fast-spreading destructive force of the element. The poem may be called a ballad for its dramatic narrative content. With a refrain that changes slightly as the action progresses, it is very close to folk poetry.

Both terms, that of a ballad and that of folk poetry, would also fit the "Die traurige Krönung" (The Sad Coronation) and "Die Tochter der Heide" (The Daughter of the Heath), which were written in 1828 and 1861. They indicate Mörike's life-long interest in English poetry. The first seems to have been in-fluenced by *Macbeth* and the other, with its initial lines "Get washed, my dear sister, get washed,/Today we go to Robin's wed-ding," points to English ballads.

But Mörike's imagination did not need to be inspired by other models. Folk poetry seemed to come as naturally to him as did mythological images. Thus the tale of "Schön-Rohtraut" (Fair Rohtraut), for example, was entirely his own invention.

Fair Rohtraut

King Ringang's daughter, what is her name?
Rohtraut, Fair Rohtraut.
How does she spend her days, and where,
When for spinning and sewing she does not care?
Goes fishing and hunting.
Her hunter I'd like to be!
Fishing and hunting would fascinate me.
—Be quiet, my heart!

And when a little while has passed,
   Rohtraut, Fair Rohtraut,
Ringang's castle is served by the lad.
A hunter's garb and horse he had.
   Goes hunting with Rohtraut.
The son of a king I would like to be!
Rohtraut, Fair Rohtraut is dear to me.
—Be quiet, my heart!

One day they rested under an oak,
   There laughs Fair Rohtraut:
"Why look at me with such delight?
Kiss me if you've the heart, young knight!"
Ah joy! How startled the lad!
And yet he thinks: "So she'll agree,"
Then kisses Fair Rohtraut lustily.
—Be quiet, my heart!

And silently the two rode home.
And on their way they didn't speak.
   Rohtraut, Fair Rohtraut;
But in his heart he would joyfully say:

"And if they made you Empress today,
't would never hurt me!
Ye leaves in the forest have seen my bliss,
Fair Rohtraut offered her lips for a kiss!
—Be quiet, my heart!"[33]

Mörike wrote the poem on March 31, 1838, but still remembered the extraordinary circumstances of its origin many years later. He wrote to the painter Moritz von Schwind:

The strongest of this kind [sudden inspiration] that I ever experienced is the origin of the ballad "Rohtraut." Once, in Cleversulzbach, I accidentally—in a dictionary—came upon the old German woman's name hitherto unknown to me. It shone at me as if in a glow of roses, and with it the princess was already there too. Warmed by this image, I stepped from the room on the ground level into the garden, went once down the path to the arbor farthest back and had invented the poem, the meter and the first lines, almost simultaneously, whereupon the composition followed quite spontaneously.[34]

It is interesting here to note the different processes that went into the making of the poem: the invention of the story, the finding of the meter, then the execution. Since Mörike stresses the rarity of their simultaneous origin, we can surmise that ordinarily he had to work at the individual elements much more consciously, a fact which was concealed by his own accounts in poems such as "At the Forest" or in *Spillner* but is revealed by a comparison of the various versions of many poems.

This question of unconscious conception or masterly construction is especially important in connection with the many poems of Mörike that have the character of folk songs. Was he really so much of a child and so close to the simple mode of thinking and of representation ascribed to primitive people that the somewhat disconnected line of thoughts and images of the folk song came to his mind spontaneously, or did he apply as much technical knowledge to such poems as to his sonnets and distichs? We can find his own answer to this question in a letter to Hartlaub from November 7, 1837: "I had a very pleasant experience I would like to relate to you right away. This morning around ten thirty I went for a walk—All at once I hear the singing of girls, several voices, from the little town, and stop. One of them, the most slender one of the three, walked in the center and sang especially clearly and boldly while marching, the others at least not wrongly."[35] Mörike continues to tell Hartlaub that he could only understand a few words but got the whole text from the servant girl when he came home. Then he writes about other matters, and only at the end of the letter does he seem to chuckle when saying: "When I told you about the little song, I pulled your leg a little. It is my own and I wrote it the other day in the morning in bed right after I woke up. I simply wanted you to read it unprejudiced (which you now did) and then tell me whether it impressed you as a folk song, or only partially so, or not at all." Thus, according to the poet, the poem "Die Schwestern" (The Sisters) owes its origin entirely to inspiration:

The Sisters

We sisters two, we fair ones,
So equal in our face,
No egg thus resembles the other,
No star the other at all.

We sisters two, we fair ones,
We both have light-brown hair,
And if you plait them in one braid
You cannot tell them apart.

We sisters two, we fair ones,
We wear an equal dress
When walking in the meadow green
And singing hand in hand.

We sisters two, we fair ones,
We both can spin so fast,
We sit at the same distaff
And sleep in the same bed.

O sisters two, you fair ones,
How has the story changed!
You both have the same sweetheart—
The song has come to its end.

(Lines two and three rhyme, in the original).

At least five other folk songs were written by Mörike during the year 1837: "Der Gärtner" (The Gardener), "Die Soldaten-braut" (The Soldier's Sweetheart), "Der Tambour" (The Drum-mer), "Suschens Vogel" (Susan's Bird), and "Jägerlied" (The Song of the Hunter). As the titles show, most of these poems are character poems; that is, Mörike projected himself into the situation of another person and expressed the latter's thoughts and feelings. These persons are not individuals with their own names and histories, but they represent entire groups; for exam-ple, that of lovers temporarily separated. Many of these songs have been set to music—some of them many times— and have been sung by many people, who did not know the author, as genuine folk songs.

While poems like the above have been the delight of Mörike's readers, another group of his folk songs has been the object of much scholarly discussion and interpretation. Many of them are concerned with the topic of the unfaithful lover and the for-saken girl. The crucial time at which knowledge of the insta-bility of love strikes man most painfully always seems to be the hour of dawn, that time of fleeting impressions between night and day, during which man is still half in dreams and thus closer to the truths of the unconscious. Most representative in this connection are two poems; the first is "Ein Stündlein wohl vor Tag":

An Hour before Daylight

When sleeping still I lay,
An hour before the day,
Outside my window on the tree
A little swallow sang to me,
An hour before the day:

"Listen to what I say!
Your sweetheart does betray.
While I am singing here to thee,
Another kisses calmly he
An hour before the day."

O woe! not further say!
Be still! And go away!

> Be gone, be gone and leave my tree!
> —O, love and faith are dreams for me
> An hour before the day.

The other poem is:

The Forsaken Girl

Early, when the cocks crow,
Before the stars expire,
To the hearth I must go,
And must light the fire.

Flames give such lovely sheen,
The sparks are leaping:
I gaze at them unseen,
My sorrows reaping.

Suddenly, faithless lad,
It comes to me,
That all this night I had
But dreams of thee.

I shed tear after tear,
Steadily flowing;
Meanwhile the day is here—
Wish, it were going![36]

In "Agnes," the state of despair after love is lost is likened to a dream. Life has become unreal, and with the loss of love the world has lost its meaning. In these poems, love is understood in an absolute sense, since to the person in grief there seems to be only that one possible love and no consolation. We are reminded of Mörike's own situation underlying the poem "On a Winter Morning," in which he too—at the moment of retardation—seemed to lose his grasp of the reality of the young day. We cannot doubt that the experience of the girl in "An Hour before the Day" was his own, that faith in love and activity could seem unreal to him before the sun began its majestic flight, but we also know that he tried to overcome such feelings. He said so very clearly in 1828 in the poem "In der Frühe" (In the Early Morning), in which he describes his condition after a sleepless night when his disturbed mind was full of doubts and created "nightly ghosts." Then, after eight lines of delving into such gloomy depths, he inserts a hyphen, turns about and tells his soul to open up to outside impressions and to rejoice, for morning bells are already ringing. Once more we encounter a certain ambiguity: day is both the time that reminds us of our losses and the time which can heal us if we accept its challenge. The brooding of the early poem "In the Open Country" and of such poems as "In the Early Morning" is overcome by the maturing poet or, at least, absent from his works, and at the end of his long list of folk poetry we find so resolved and calm a poem as "Denk es, o Seele!" (Think of It, O Soul), which the poet placed at the end of his Mozart novella:

> A little fir tree greens somewhere,
> Who knows, deep in the forest,
> A rose-bush, who can tell us,
> In what garden?
> They have been chosen yet,
> Think of it, O soul!
> To take roots in your grave
> And there to grow.

> And two black ponies pasture
> On the meadow,
> Return then home to town
> Happily leaping.
> They will walk step by step
> Once with your body;
> Perhaps, perhaps before yet
> From their hoofs
> The shoe comes loose
> That I see sparkle there.[37]

IV *Mörike's Love Poetry*

The only poem written at Urach which the poet allowed to be published is, "Erinnerung" (Recollection). It reflects his love for his cousin Klara. Playing on three different time levels, it blends the time of their childhood games with that of their adolescence, which saw them part from each other, and the time at which the poem was written, when the poet wishes to return to the earlier times. Each period is illustrated by an idyllic scene described in simple and naïve language. The unrhymed trochaic meter, with four stresses per line, flows swiftly without effort, as in these last lines of the poem:

> And I asked you for the rose
> You were wearing on your bosom,
> And with timid eyes you quickly
> Gave it to me while we walked:
> Trembling to my lips I put it,
> Kissed it hotly two or three times;
> Nobody could jest about it,
> Not a soul did see me do it,
> And you did not watch yourself.
>
> At the people's house to whom I
> Had been asked to chaperon you,
> We stopped still, remember, I
> Pressed your hand and—
> This then was the very last time,
> That I went with you, o Klara!
> It is true, that was the last time
> We were happy just like children.

"Der junge Dichter" (The Young Poet) of the year 1823 speaks of the poet's problems. Calling himself a son of Apollo still under age and not able to find poetic expression for the wealth nature and life are showering upon him, he admits that he is often given to despair. At such moments he finds relief when sitting down with his beloved and listening to her loving words. Then it may even happen to him that he wishes to forget all about his poetic endeavors.

But Mörike's poetic power was growing, as we can see from the poem "Nächtliche Fahrt" (A Ride at Night) written during the same year. This is a much more complex poem than "Der junge Dichter" (The Young Poet). In its first version, it was called "Dream" because it traces the succession of pictures that had occurred to the narrator in a dream. In the dream he feels swiftly taken by carriage through a strange countryside until he comes to the village of his unfaithful sweetheart. Upon leaving the village, he sees a beggar girl standing next to the carriage and quickly throws her the necklace he once received from his sweetheart. Suddenly the carriage is stopped, and the beautiful girl takes him by the hand saying: "So I discover your treason.

I shall not forgive it before you, in turn, are good to me again."
She caresses him and cries like one who is doing repentance. He
remains silent but cannot help feeling happy in her embrace,
wishing that the horses would go on forever and morning would
never come. The figures of the sweetheart and the beggar girl
are so curiously mingled in this poem that literary historians
have asked themselves whether it does not give the first poetic
account of Maria Meyer's impression on Mörike. Perhaps Klara
and Maria are fused here as the sweetheart and the beggar girl.
The approach to the guilt problem definitely appears like a pre-
lude to the poems of the Peregrina cycle, which became the reflection of the poet's inner struggles caused by his love for Maria.

The Peregrina cycle consists of five very different poems. The
first of these consists only of one stanza in *ottava rima*. Numbers
two and three are in free verse; number four is rhymed but with
lines of different length; and the last one is a sonnet. The image
of the beloved also changes throughout the cycle. In the first
poem she is called an unknowing child who harbors sacred
grief. At the end of the next poem, she is the strange child, in
the following a slender, fairy-like girl, then an image of pitiable
but beautiful pain; and in the last poem she is Love herself,
beautiful in her madness, jesting, with wild wreaths wound in
her hair. Through all these variations the concept of her innocence runs like a red thread. Even when she offers the poet a
"cup of sins" in the first poem, she does so unknowingly. If she
shows essentially so little change, the development in the poems
must be derived from the character of the lover. To trace his
changing attitude toward the girl, we must look at all the poems
somewhat more closely.

The first poem only gives a picture of the girl who seems to invite the poet to Love fused with Death and Sin, while the second
contains much more action. It is the description of a wedding
celebration, a very unusual celebration, indeed. The setting is
fantastic and exotic and may have been influenced by a similar
description in Justinus Kerner's works.[38] An open tent is carried by twelve iron columns in the shape of snakes. The bride is
brought to the tent in silent procession. She wears a black dress
and a red scarf. Smiling, she sits down to the delicious meal.

[58]

At this point, the poet changes to the past tense. He relates how the lovers stole away from the crowd into the garden where roses were burning and the moonshine lay on the lilies. The trees half covered the pond. Here, on the grass, they rested and he smothered her with kisses. Next to them, the fountain was splashing and they did not heed the friendly voices and the music in the distance. Sooner than the lover could wish, the bride feels tired. Holding her in his lap, he still caresses her softly, touching her eyes with his own and feeling her eyelashes go up and down like the wings of butterflies.

Only at the end of the night, just before dawn, did he awaken her to lead her into his house. We know that this poetic account differs from what really happened: Mörike had not taken Maria Meyer into his house. His poetic imagination was inspired here not by reality but possibly by his readings and most likely, by wishes he had suppressed. Perhaps he had experienced such fulfillment in his dreams. Or possibly he was telling himself what he should have done.

What really happened is poetically expressed in the next poem, "Peregrina III,"

> Disturbance entered the moon-lit gardens
> Of a once sacred love.
> I shuddered at finding deceit in the past
> And with crying eyes, yet cruelly,
> I bid the slender
> Enchanting girl
> To go away from me.
> O, her noble head
> Was bent low, for she loved me;
> But she went in silence
> Into the gray
> World out there.
>
> Sick ever since,
> And hurt, and filled with grief is my heart.
> Never will it recover!
> As if, spun out of air, a magic thread
> Were binding us, an anxious tie,
> I am drawn, drawn after her by my love!
> —What? If I found her one day on my threshold

Sitting there, as before, in the morning-twilight,
Her travelling bundle beside her,
And her eye, looking up at me loyally,
Said to me: See, I have come
Back from the wide world![39]

Almost every line of this poem calls for comment. The word
"disturbance" in the first line, for example, stands for the German word *Irrsal*, a word often used by the poet Hölderlin, who
exerted considerable influence on Mörike at that time. *Irrsal*
could be translated by such words as "error" or "madness." In
addition, it implies a certain helplessness on the part of the person it befalls, which is stressed by its use as the subject of the
line. The *Irrsal* came into the gardens of love as if on its own
accord and not through any fault of the lovers. Such meaning,
however, is neutralized by the word *verjährt*—"superannuated"
(past)—in the next line and the word "cruelly" in line four. Here
the speaker passes a verdict on his own behavior, declaring that
he had no right to punish the girl for a crime of the past. To a
certain extent, his situation may be called tragic because he himself had been caught in the net of conventional standards which
demand "Purity" of an unmarried girl. And he suffered as much
as the girl when he sent her away into the "gray world." This
expression forms a stark contrast to the "house" at the end of the
previous poem on the one hand and to the "wide world" in the
last line of the present one on the other. It offers neither the
protection of the home nor the enrichment of the "wide world"
and its freedom. The "gray world" is dangerous and oppressive.
And it was cruel to send the girl who loved him out into it.[40]

The next poem expands the idea already mentioned in the
third: that she might return. But what was just a thought there
now becomes a dream. The lover dreams that she has come back,
looking like the very image of grief which is asking for pity. For
a while they sit together like strangers, trying to suppress their
sorrow. Finally he breaks into loud sobbing, and then they
leave the house together, hand in hand. Thus the poet reverses
in this dream the decision of Mörike, the man. Instead of sav-
ing his protected existence, he follows his love into the world.

The last poem, a sonnet, indicates by its form that the poet was already striving for greater objectivity. He tried to deduce a general truth from his personal experience: love is tied to the pillory, from which it walks away, poor, disturbed, and without shoes. Its noble head can find no place to rest. It has to wash the wounds on its feet with tears. In the second stanza, we learn that the speaker had found Peregrina just like this, beautiful in her madness and love. He asks himself how he could ever have left such beauty and finds the consoling answer: so that it would return even more enchanting. But in the end he finds that she turns away from him never to come back.

In this poem the girl's name Peregrina is mentioned for the first time. It means the wandering girl, the girl without a home. The name is thus a condensation of the content not only of this poem but of the entire cycle. Such love as is described in the first poem—deep, mysterious, alluring, and dangerous—has no permanent place among men. This is due partly to man's inadequacy, partly to the character of love itself.

The Peregrina poems are not only deep in meaning and beautiful in form and imagery but also interesting in regard to the poet's creative process. The poems were written at different times, and they underwent considerable changes as the poet's own judgment of the real events developed. There seems to have been a turning point in his attitude in the year 1828. During his short stay in Scheer on the Danube, which occurred in that year, Mörike experienced a new love, for a schoolmaster's daughter. We do not know much about this love, but a few poems which were inspired by it indicate that the poet was deeply stirred. The experience made him think about love again and re-evaluate his former behavior. This is quite obvious in the earlier version of the last poem, the sonnet, which is dated June 19, 1828. The line that was to offer the name Peregrina in the later versions reads in this earlier form: "Recently I also found Love like this." This must have referred to the girl in Scheer rather than Maria Meyer.[41] Both experiences were subsequently fused in the figure of Peregrina.

A closer look at the first poem reveals a similar combination. The brown-eyed girl in the published eight lines was not Maria Meyer but also the girl in Scheer. Only the unpublished second stanza referred to the earlier experience: "Once upon a time a dream of wonderful life/Let me see the gold growing deep down in the earth,/It made me understand the secret powers of life which weave/In deep shafts./I felt the urge to go down, I could not resist/And below I stopped as in despair,—/I could not see the golden veins anywhere,/And a shudder full of longing was around me."[42] This poem was probably written in 1828 also. Poem number four may also belong to this period.[43]

A very different date of inception has been established for the third poem, however.[44] It exists in the form of a manuscript from Hartlaub's hand which is dated July 6, 1824. This means that the poem must have been written at the time when Maria Meyer returned to Tübingen and appealed to Mörike for help which he refused. The concurrence of Maria's presence with the inception of the poem is reflected in the following line of the manuscript version: "Am I to place my hand into her white hand?/Does not her eye pray/Saying: Here I have come again/From the wide world?"[45] The use of the present tense indicates that Mörike wrote these lines while he was still struggling with his answer to Maria's plea for help. But if the poem was created at such a moment, it shows that Mörike's poetic power was great enough to allow him to break through any personal concern and to transpose his experiences onto the level of poetry, not only in retrospect but at the very time of the happenings.

The lines of the early version are preceded by the rendering of a dream the poet had between the time of "the disturbance" and Maria's return. He saw a dark curtain between himself and the dark world. Behind the curtain he sensed a heather country. Sometimes he heard sounds of night winds, and the folds of the curtain began to move in the storm. Then the storm subsided, and suddenly the head of the girl with the magic power looked out of the slit in the curtain. Mörike removed this dream only in 1867, which marks the very end of the development the Peregrina poems underwent. The change from the present tense to the past in the last lines of the poem had been made much earlier, namely for the first edition of *Nolten the Painter,* in which the whole cycle was inserted. One year earlier, in 1831, Mörike had included the poem in a manuscript he wanted to give away as a present. In this manuscript we find the line: "I shuddered at finding deceit in the past" and the words "yet cruelly" of the next line for the first time. They were not part of the early version of 1824. And we may surmise that they were also a result of Mörike's different evaluation of the events in 1828, which was the result of his new love for the girl in Scheer. The process of re-evaluation continued and eventually came to influence also the second poem.

It was not until 1844 that Mörike wrote the lines which describe the slumbering girl and the poet's caresses. Until then, the conclusion of the poem had been much shorter and the situation very different. The girl had played the active part and the lover had fallen asleep. The exact lines read as follows: "And now standing still she went/Over my temple with her finger while her glance was strange./All at once I sank into deep slumber/But strengthened by wonderful sleep/I awakened for happy days,/Led the strange bride into my house."[46] If Mörike exchanged the roles of the characters later, he must have wanted to give a more conventional description of the relationship, although it appears almost improper now that the active lover did not lead the girl into his house much earlier. Only now has the man become the guilty one, and the image of the girl has lost the indications of magic powers. Only now has she become the innocent girl throughout the cycle.

The few poems which reflect Mörike's love for the girl in Scheer on the Danube are characterized by a particularly sensuous ring. The poet never really suppressed his delight in the physical side of love; he never strove for "Platonic" poetry, as Goethe did during his relationship with Frau von Stein. On the contrary, Mörike always appears relaxed in giving voice to the enjoyment of beauty and the senses. This seems only natural in the case of a poet of such sensitivity. And for the unmarried vicar and curate of so many years his poetry may have been a means of expressing his erotic dreams and suppressed desires.[47]

In the poem "Nimmersatte Liebe" (Insatiable Love), Mörike describes love very lightly. Comparing it with a sieve which can never be filled with water, he shows that kisses will never quench or satisfy Love. It will forever produce strange and fresh desires. Thus, for example, the girl whom the speaker kisses today remains still when he hurts her lips, and her eyes ask for more. The poem ends in a jingle repeating its very first words: "Just so is love! 't was always so,/As long as love existed,/And even old king Salomo,/The wise one, never resisted."[48]

Several of the poems which grew out of the Scheer experience have one theme in common, that of the sudden awakening of a hitherto innocent girl to the sensations of love. In the poem "Liebesvorzeichen" (Predictions of Love), this transition is described as parallel to the change in nature when the buds burst into bloom. At the beginning of the poem, the girl is still joking like a child and the pomegranate tree is still in bud, both unaware of their closeness to being kissed and to flowering. On the next morning, the blossoms are open, and when the boy takes this for a good sign and meets the girl hopefully, he finds her already waiting. And they will still be kissing after the tree has stopped flowering.

The short poem ("Josephine"), which was published only in 1864, concentrates on the girl's situation just a little later when she has already "enjoyed happiness," but this still remains a secret for everybody but the speaker. In the form of an epigram, the poet now pokes fun at those who still think that this girl is just growing up for the first expressions of love. The four lines of this poem are almost identical with a few lines from a longer poem, "Götterwink" (Hint of the Gods), that was written in 1845.[49] H. Maync has attributed this poem to Mörike's love for his later wife, Margarete, and has suggested that the epigram was lifted from the longer poem. Krummacher, however, doubts that "Hint of the Gods" could have referred to Margarete just a few months after the Mörikes had met her. We may, therefore, suggest a reversal of the origin of the two poems. Josephine was the name Mörike used for the girl in Scheer in another poem we have yet to discuss. We could then take the title of the epigram seriously and assume a much earlier date for the writing of the four lines than the date of their publication. Indeed, the poem may have been another early version which the poet withheld. But it was fertile ground he had touched here, and slowly the poem "Hint of the Gods" grew out of it—a poem that satisfied the highest demands the poet made on himself.

The poem describes the poet waiting outside a hall in which his sweetheart is dancing. The flowers in the garden surrounding him are in bloom. He can hear the gaiety of the dancers and, slowly, he becomes anxious and jealous of those who can dance with her. To console himself he seems to speak to those dancers, telling them that all their courting must be in vain since he himself has already secretly kissed her. Talking like this to himself, he unnoticeably increases his own longing and is again in need of something that would calm him. This time Nature answers his yearning: Suddenly a light, like that of a torch, quickly moves behind the nocturnal window in the gallery, strongly shines over to him and makes the rose stand out in high glow from the dark bushes next to him. He hails the flower that foretells the happiness which is in store for him. His heart beats faster, and a thoughtful statement again draws the conclusion from the poem: "The call of the demonic powers is deeply stirring even if it promises victory."⁵⁰

The poem "Hint of the Gods" is written in distichs just as "In the Park" and "The Beautiful Beech Tree" are. It should really be discussed together with Mörike's poems in classical meter of the 1840's. The treatment of love may, however, justify this discussion in connection with poems like "Predictions of Love" and "Insatiable Love," which also concentrate on sensual desires.

The other poem, "Josephine," which can be dated June 1828, is rather different in character. Religious feelings are here fused with erotic ones. The poem starts with the description of a Catholic Mass. The morning sun is breaking through the incense and the priest has stopped speaking when the poet hears the choir sing. Its singing plunges from the gallery like an eagle who is intoxicated by the sun and, like Jove's coat, comes down from the clouds. He can distinguish one voice in the choir. This beautiful voice seems to nestle up to the sound of the flute. It belongs to a girl who stands very modestly and shyly on the gallery. The poet steps behind her, touches her dress, feels close to her. He speaks to her and describes her reaction with rising exultation. First he speaks of her brown eyes shyly covered by the lids, then of her mouth which had just sung of God and talked to him in such simple manner. The tone of her voice sinks into his heart and makes it fall ill. He stands as in a dream while the organ-playing stops, the girl passes him, the service breaks up, and the candles waver.[51] Could it be that this religious atmosphere also influenced the poet when he spoke of sin in connection with love in the stanza of the first Peregrina poem which stems from the Scheer experience?

In the spring of 1830, Mörike's love for Luise Rau found expression in a number of poems. These are not linked so closely as to be called a cycle, yet they do belong together, as is indicated by their first publication, with the exception of "Liebesglück" (Happiness of Love), in the novel *Nolten the Painter.* They are also identified as a group by their form: they are all sonnets. Mörike had used this form in the last Peregrina poem, but the other poems of that cycle were in free verse or followed a rhyme scheme without a definite stanzaic pattern. The German sonnet always consists of two quatrains and two tercets, and appears to restrain the content more than free verse, for example. Goethe had used it in 1807/8 to give shape to the expression of a love strong enough to be compared to the waters of a mountain stream plunging down from the heights which he wanted to restrain and possibly overcome. The superiority of mind displayed in Goethe's sonnets gives to several of them a touch of playfulness and self-irony.

This is also true of Mörike's poems of the year 1830. The poem "At the Forest," which usually introduces the group, especially reflects Mörike's attitude to society in a very serene manner. Lying in the grass at the edge of the forest, he is happy to have escaped being annoyed by the foolishness of society. The last lines read: "And if the noble people only knew/How beautifully poets waste their time/They might even envy me./For the closely wound wreaths of the sonnet/Form by themselves under my hands,/While my eyes are feasting in the distance."[52] In the other sonnets, the theme of his new love is related to his concern with creativity. At first glance, the poem "Happiness of Love" seems to be rather nonchalant when the poet graciously suggests that we forgive those poets who invent their lines about love's happiness rather than speak from experience. He then rejoices that he really did find happiness with his graceful and innocent girl and stresses how different this new love is from one he had experienced earlier. That earlier love had brought him only trouble and bitterness. His happy song comes to an end with an apparent witticism. The poet admits that the contrast between him and those poets who describe an unreal situation does not actually exist. His happiness often seems so immeasurably great to him that it also appears unreal and he feels as if in a dream.

The poet feels equally overwhelmed by his love in the sonnet "Zu viel" (Too Much). It begins with a scene similar to that in the poem "In Spring": The hill in spring longs for the light of the sky; the previously benumbed world melts into the blessing of love and takes on the form of a delicate poem. At the slope near the pine tree stands the house of the narrator's sweetheart —so far the external situation is described. A new phase of the poem follows in which the poet seems to weigh the meaning all this beauty has for him. Love and Nature are both so overwhelming that he calls on the one to help him bear the other. We are reminded of the poem "At Night," where he was overcome by the beauty of the night. In "Too Much," however, night is summoned to help the poet recover from the strong impressions of the day. Its mild stars promise divine coolness. And the poet descends into the depths of meditation. For "depths" he uses the word *Abgrund*, which is usually translated as abyss, and which, like the English word, can be used with or without pejorative meaning. Love and Nature have brought about a creative moment.

The transition to the next poem "Nur zu!" (Go Ahead) is like the sudden revival in the last stanza of "On a Winter Morning." The rose blooms as if it were never to wither; the eagle strives upward, not asking whether it will hit his head against a ceiling; and love must go ahead although it is not assured of happiness.

The final poem once more combines many of the themes contained in the others: from happiness of the speaker about having found such a sweetheart, through fear that all may be a dream, to a plunge into the depths where he can hear the springs of fate murmur melodiously, and, finally, to a lifting up of the face to the stars.

The poem which takes the place of "Happiness in Love" in the novel *Nolten the Painter* begins with a melancholic glance into the past but offers reassurance to remind us of the eternal light which will dissolve all passions. The eternal also plays a role in the variation of the last line in "Go Ahead" as included in the novel: love may venture the flight into the eternal. These changes may have been conditioned by the context of the poems in *Nolten,* where they are the last treasure of the painter's fiancée before her sick mind guides her to her death. They are followed by a religious poem "Karwoche" (During Passion Week).

Among Mörike's unpublished manuscripts, another sonnet with the title "An Luise" (To Luise) was found. It is similar to a poem which the poet published in 1852 under the title "An M." (To M.). Mörike had revised the poem to Luise Rau to make it fit Margarete Speeth. He was now describing a very different character. While Luise, according to the poem, had fulfilled her duties cheerfully with an even temper, Margarete often showed herself adverse to those around her. She hides the treasures of her heart and yet she is a proof that truth, virtue, love, and faithfulness have not yet left this earth. And what she herself believes lost—blissful peace—is also closer to her than she thinks. After reading this poem, nobody should say that Mörike did not know what he ventured in a union with so difficult a person.

He must have been convinced that love, as he expressed it in the poem "Aus der Ferne" (From Afar) in 1846 could overcome such adversity. The poem is a dialogue between a man and a woman. The opening lines are twice repeated in other stanzas: "Blow, O blow, ye morning winds!/Carry a word of love hither and thither"; and once they appear in a varied form: "Quiet, be quiet now, ye morning winds/Blow again tomorrow in the morning," at the end. All lines are in trochaic pentameter, a meter not too frequently used in German literature, since it does not flow as easily as iambic verse. In this particular poem the disadvantage of the meter is overcome by the exclusive use of feminine endings. The setting of the poem is a mixture of exotic elements (as the riding of the mule, the bottle of balm hanging from a necklace of corals), reminders of medieval times (the hall, the hawk, the harp, and the balcony from which girls watch the men in armor), and a regional expression (*Höckerweib=*

[68]

woman with hunchback). Perhaps Mörike tried to follow in the footsteps of Goethe who just as anachronistically had mixed references to different cultures in his "West-Östlicher Divan" (West-Eastern Divan). Certainly, this poem indicates a stronger concern with form and setting than with depth of thought and feeling. Mörike did not address many poems to Margarete. Those which he wrote during the time of their betrothal and marriage return to the subject of nature, describe objects of art, or invoke idyllic scenes. The poems do not reflect his own life troubled with ill health or, later, with marital problems but bear witness to the poet's imagination, power of observation, and his sense of humor.

V *Mörike's Classicism*

We have had occasion to observe Mörike's romantic inclinations and his *Biedermeier* tendencies. We have also noticed that in some poems he was a forerunner of the *poésie pure* of the French Symbolists. But all these terms encompass only a part of Mörike's poetry. They cannot do justice to a number of poems which belong in the framework of classical tradition. The poet was not only an admirer of ancient poets and a translator of poems from antiquity; many of his own works are conceived in the classical spirit. They fathom the depth of human experience—that of Death, for example, in the poem "Erinna," and that of Love and its demonic undertone in "Hint of the Gods"—but instead of becoming lost in bottomless darkness as he did in the first Peregrina poem, the poet now brings the gold to the surface. He is so preoccupied with form and beauty that we must relate his striving to that of Goethe and Schiller. His classical creed is stated in the following letter: "Form in its deepest meaning is quite inseparable from content; indeed, in its origin it is almost in unison with it and of a completely spiritual, highly delicate nature. I do not ask for correctness as long as there is beauty. A beautiful thought, and a beautiful sentiment can be revealed poetically only by beautiful form...."[53]

Mörike had been prepared for the classical forms from early youth. Schools at that time stressed a knowledge of ancient writers and used their works as models for the students' exercises. But Mörike was to do more than that. In 1840 he edited a

Classische Blumenlese (Anthology of Classical Poetry) in translation; in 1855 he prepared eleven idyls by Theocritus for an edition his friend Friedrich Notter was to publish, and in 1864 he occupied himself with a new publication of *Anakreon und die sogenannten Anakreontischen Lieder* (Anacreon and the So-Called Anacreontics).[54] In each case he did not furnish completely new translations but made use of the existing ones, justifying this method in a foreword by saying that translations may reach a certain level of excellence which cannot be surpassed, and that it would be foolish to meddle with them.[55] He did make some changes, however, where he thought they constituted an improvement. In two instances, his translations were so new that he did not hesitate to include the poems, "Akme und Septimius" (Akme and Septimus) and "Auf den Arrius" (About Arrius) (both adaptations of poems by Catullus), in his own works. What counts for us here is mainly the fact of his very intimate acquaintance with classical poetry.

Mörike's classicism is reflected in his own works from 1835 on. Almost all the poems to be discussed in the present chapter are in hexameter, in distichs, or trimeter. These forms were, of course, not a goal in themselves but simply the mirror of Mörike's inner striving for balance and restraint. Such striving had been present very early, as is shown by a sonnet from 1828. In this poem, he had posed the question: who among the modern poets was still a master of the ancient art? The only one Mörike could think of then was Goethe; and he predicted the end of an era with Goethe's death. He could not know at that time that in a few decades he himself would be called "a son of Horace and a delicate Swabian" by Gottfried Keller, or that another contemporary, Paul Heyse, would say that "a touch of Goethe and the Greeks surrounded him."

From 1835 on, Mörike acknowledged his indebtedness to the ancient poets in short poems on authors like Theocritus or Tibullus.[56] But as early as 1831 he had attested the strong influence which Goethe and Homer alike could have on his striving for balance.[57] Other persons to whom he addressed poems and for whom he felt admiration or thankfulness included the astronomer Kepler, the poet Hölty, Schiller's mother (who was buried in Cleversulzbach), personal friends, and also his physician. At this point, it may be appropriate to remember that the poetry of these years was wrought from a suffering body. There is no hint of this in the often light-hearted, always graceful verses.

Some of the poems show a similarity with those of the Anacreontic poets of the eighteenth century, who had followed the same ancient models. But while they had hardly shown any depth in their concern with love, drinking, and singing, and used Greek or Roman mythological or literary figures, such as Diana and Amor or the Graces and the Horæ, in a purely decorative manner, Mörike renewed ancient themes and symbols and restored their deeper meaning. Knowing, for example, Mörike's experience of the flow of time, we can see his striving to understand the sense of this phenomenon and to accept it in the following lines to the goddesses of the seasons from 1846, entitled "Inschrift auf eine Uhr mit den drei Horen":

Inscription on a Clock with the Three Horæ

"The horæ stride slowly ahead of other blissful gods."
Theocritus

We do most slowly stride of all the gods,
We silent ones, richly adorned with crowns of leaves.
For him who honors us and whom we give our favor,
Since he loves gracefulness and sacred moderation,
Before his eyes in gentle dance we move,
And bring variation into his long day.

Gracefulness and moderation were Mörike's ideals during his later years. These lines about the hours stand out in German literature because of their form. Mörike used the trimeter here, which is hard to achieve in German or in English. In the German, the trimeter consists of a line with six stresses. The meter should be iambic or, in exceptional cases, dactylic. Since German lacks longer adjectives, Goethe, for example, refrained from using this form. In the above translation, only lines two, three, and four reproduce the form Mörike used.

We find the same form in one of Mörike's most widely discussed poems, "Auf eine Lampe":

To a Lamp

Still undisturbed, o lovely lamp, you decorate,
So delicately hung up here on your light chains,
The ceiling of the now almost forgotten room.
On your white marble bowl along the rim of which
The brazen wreath of ivy golden-green is wrought
A happy crowd of children dances in a ring.
All is so charming! Laughing, yet a gentle touch
Of seriousness is poured out over the entire form—
A piece of art of the true kind! Who pays it heed?
But what is beautiful $\begin{cases} \text{shines} \\ \text{seems} \end{cases}$ blissful in itself.[58]

We can easily see why the trimeter was no problem for Mörike. The poem abounds in descriptive words. Many of them
are derived from verb forms and thus make the poem dramatic,
even though it is the description of an object that does not
change. Expressions like "still undisturbed," "almost forgotten,"
"hung up," "wrought," and "poured around" all create a sense
of action. The choice of adjectives in this poem is also reveal-
ing. It conveys to us Mörike's theory of beauty. Words like
"gentle," "happy," "golden-green," "white," "graceful," and
"light" all describe certain aspects of that one quality: beauty.
According to this poem, it consists of playful gracefulness and a
soft seriousness.

The particular problem of the poem lies in its last two lines.
Pensively the poet states: A genuine piece of art. Who pays attention to it? But whatever is beautiful . . . blissful in itself. The
word just omitted is the equivalent of the German word
scheinen, which could be translated either by "to shine"$=$ to
give off light or by "to seem"$=$ it seems, i.e., it looks like it; but
we cannot be sure. Emil Staiger used the latter meaning to support his theory that Mörike was a person who came late in the
intellectual development of Germany, the climax of which
Staiger finds in Goethe. In Staiger's opinion, Mörike could
only surmise and suspect the essence of life. Goethe saw the
eternal idea of beauty in the individual beautiful object and
was not haunted by the knowledge of its frailty. Mörike, however, had lost the assurance of certain values, among them
beauty.

Staiger's interpretation was at once disputed by other literary historians and by Martin Heidegger. Heidegger reads the word *scheinen* as meaning "to give off light" and finds that the melancholy of the poem issues not from uncertainty about the existence of beauty but from the realization that it is often overlooked.[59] Since the beginning of the controversy in 1951 there have been other attempts to arrive at an understanding of Mörike's intentions in the last line. Some critics point to Schiller's theory of *schöner Schein* (beautiful appearance) and to a poem by Theocritus that may have influenced Mörike.[60] The most promising approach may yet be that of relating the doubtful line to other Mörike poems.[61]

One poem especially seems to be closely related to "To a Lamp." It is called "Corinna" and deals with a girl who dances the round dance with her sisters so gracefully, unconscious of the complete unison of her soul and figure, that she makes the observer wish to be like her: "O, to the person whose entire being and life/would move through the circle of the years like this,/being in lovely balance at each moment,/as a blissful satisfaction for himself/and gladdening and edifying all others!" It is true, Corinna is not "almost forgotten," but to her that does not really matter. It is most important that she is *Sich selber so zu seliger Genüge* (such a blissful satisfaction for herself). This may well be the meaning of the last line in "To a Lamp" also. It is unlikely that Mörike should not have been aware of the meaning of the verb to shine in a poem about a lamp. Students of English literature must also notice the strong resemblance of the poem with Keats's similar endeavors as, for example, in the "Ode on a Grecian Urn." But in Keats's poems beauty exists in itself.

How strongly Mörike could experience the actual existence of beauty we know also from such poems as "The Beautiful Beech Tree" and "Hint of the Gods." In the last poem, he used the rose as a symbol for beauty and love. This symbol appears also in a poem of truly dionysian character that portrays the poet's intoxication through an encounter with beauty. In this poem, "Auf einer Wanderung" (On an Excursion), the speaker comes to a small, friendly town, where the rosy glow of the evening sun lies in the streets. He stops in front of a window from which he hears singing float out like the golden sounds of bells. One voice carries more beautifully than the others; it resembles a choir of nightingales and makes the flowers in front of the window sway, the air swing, and the roses glow in a deeper red. Unaware of his path, the poet wanders out of the city and there, outside, finds the world gleaming brightly, the sky surging up in purple, and the city behind him in a golden haze. The sounds of the brook and the mill in the valley touch his ear—he feels elated, led astray, and he rejoices: "O Muse, you have touched my heart with a breath of love!"

This is a very extraordinary poem. Written twenty years after the Peregrina cycle, it still conveys the ardor and involvement of the early poems written in free verse. At a time when most of his poetry was in classical meter, Mörike could yet be touched by nature. The rustling of the brooks and alders and of the mill in the vale remind us of his inclination to "romantic" spots and folk-song scenes. The repeated use of the word "gold" brings back the images of the first Peregrina poem, where gold was the symbol for the luring and dangerous treasures the girl—and through her, love—had to offer. In "On an Excursion," gold is characteristic of the wealth of the human voice—which is also compared to the ringing of bells—and of the overflowing glow of nature, which wraps the city in a golden haze.

An earlier version of the poem did not contain the lines about the golden city. The earlier version is a lengthy description, in a humorous tone, of the wanderings of two friends who compare this voice from the window to others they have heard before. Mörike replaced it in a manuscript collection, which he had started in 1844, by the new poem "On an Excursion" at the same time that he sent this new version to Hartlaub in a letter of August 22 and 30, 1845, with the remark: "An old piece changed at a good hour."[62] This "good hour" was not the moment at which he may have heard the beautiful voice but the time he was again inspired by his earlier lines. Only then did he create the vision of the golden city, the rustling brook and the alders, and gave thanks to the Muse who had bestowed this vision upon him. When he wrote these lines, he did not see the city before him; it was in himself like the images in his soul he had mentioned in "On a Winter Morning." He did not deal with it as a past experience but impresses us with such an immediacy of expression that we seem to share his vision.

"On an Excursion" was not the first poem to voice Mörike's sensitivity to music, which existed since his early youth. During the Cleversulzbach years, he often visited the Hartlaubs, and Wilhelm Hartlaub must have played the piano at Mörike's behest. In the poem "To Wilhelm Hartlaub" (1842), the poet expressed his thanks for the hours they had spent together. He described the wandering of his mind while the friend played. First it seemed to lead him along black depths where the singing of the hidden springs could be heard, then it changed and reflected the blue extended sky with a host of stars. Now the poet's mind wanders to the player: At once a beam of joy pierces him: suddenly the whole worth of his friend becomes clear. Then he begins to think. He finds it wonderful that love and loyalty between friends still exist and that, in all the abundance of life, they are kept together in the enjoyment of a present they are sure of. But he is unable to express his gratitude at once, so the poem continues. His silent search for words comes to an end when—in the final stanza—Hartlaub's daughter invites her father and the poet to the table. In an idyllic scene they all gather for a simple meal while the evening bells are ringing to signify the end of the day's loveliness.

VI *The Idyllic Mood*

The idyllic mood of "The Beautiful Beech Tree" already received our attention in the introductory chapter. It served as an example for the achievement of the mature Mörike of the 1840's. By that time, his earlier experiences of the dangerous depths of love or nature, and of the transitoriness of life, were restrained by his striving for clarity and harmony. Only the term "demonic quiet" in the poem about the beech tree reminds us of the hidden magic powers. In a number of poems, even such allusions are missing. These poems are entirely idyllic.

This complete lack of a tragic element or of problematic character in some of his poems was the cause of much misunderstanding in Mörike's own time and in most recent scholarship. Some of his contemporaries read the idyllic poetry as a record of his personal life and overlooked the darker sides of his existence, while modern scholars refer to Wispel and to "the Trusty Man" as masks of the poet who was not sure of his own identity. They interpret the idyllic country parson of "The Old Weathercock" or the wanderer who speaks congenially to his old boots in the "Erbauliche Betrachtung" (Edifying Contemplation) as roles of a poet who tried to close his eyes to the abyss in order to maintain his inner balance. With such an attitude it is hard to give these poems due consideration. Biographical interpretation stands in the way of esthetic judgment. What matters here, after all, is the degree to which content and form have united to bring about a perfect piece of art. We may also ask ourselves the extent to which Mörike was able to keep alive the idyllic genre, which he admired so much in the writings of classical poets whose works he translated.

To take these poems seriously thus does not mean that we make the mistake of Mörike's earliest readers who believed the parson in "The Old Weathercock" to be Mörike himself. We know from one of his letters to Theodor Storm that he consciously transposed the parson onto the level of a family man, endowing him with wife and children and moving him into an earlier historical period, in order to let him appear more dignified. He had begun the poem when the old weathercock was removed from the church tower in Cleversulzbach and picked up by the poet, who took it to his own yard in 1840. The first version consisted of only twenty-two verses in which the weathercock himself reported the happenings. It was expanded a little in 1845 after Mörike had moved to Mergentheim and taken the weathercock along. He now added the idea that the cock was planted on the stove in the parson's study. The poem—293 lines in all—was finished in 1852, that is, long after Mörike's own life as a country parson and, as he also says in the letter to Storm, out of longing for such a life. We know that he did not feel that the profession had been his real calling at the time; but nevertheless he had spent many fine hours in Cleversulzbach.

Yet Mörike was not like the parson in the poem. That parson gives no indication of interests other than his profession, and it is in his work that the weathercock observes him from the oven. But we see not only the parson in his various occupations, we also hear about the stories depicted on the tiles around the oven of Belshazzar and of Abraham and Sarah—and we hear of the weathercock's nightly thoughts about the welfare of the villagers. The entire atmosphere is that of a childlike naïveté, fairy tale-like with a brief touch of the possibility of evil—robbers may be at work somewhere else during the night—and the deep feeling that all is well with this world. Because of its humor and its form of doggerel, the poem belongs to the tradition of Hans Sachs's poetry, which Goethe had only recently praised.

Mörike did not use doggerel very often. Most of the poems to be discussed here are in classical meter. They are concerned with such simple phenomena as the life of country people and their closeness to the settings of fairy tales. They are humorous when, for example, the mosquitoes distract the poet from such lofty readings as Klopstock's *Odes,* or the melodious sounds from a garden gate remind him of a Mozart opera. It is as if he had returned from his flights into the extraordinary to the common life that has not changed since the time when Catullus or Theocritus employed the same forms. The little scenes in these poems reveal an eternal truth. In their longing for a simple life some of them are close to the works of many ancient writers of a later period. Such thoughts are clearly expressed at the end of "Wald-Idylle" (Forest Idyl):

Friend, you honor the muse, who sang fairy tales by the thousands
    Probably long ago; now she is silent, though,
Who at the warm fireplace, at the carver's bench or the loom oft'
    Precious nourishment gave to the poetical mind.
Her field is the impossible; bold, lighthearted, she ties up
    Things that lie far apart; gaily rewards the fool.
Given three wishes her hero will choose the thing that's most silly.
    I want to honor her; therefore let me confess,
How there next to the girl, the talkative one, quite softly
    Into my deeply moved heart ardently entered the wish:
Had I been born as a hunter, a shepherd or possibly farmer,
    I would carry the stick and the axe, Margreth would be my wife!
Never would I complain about the heat and would gladly
    Also eat coarser food, if it were brought here by you.
O how splendidly would the sun every morning appear to
    Me and the evening glow over the ripening field!

Balsam my blood would become in the hearty kiss of the woman,
  Strongly my house would grow, doubly, in children, to bloom.
But in the winter, at night, when the snow drifts outside, at the oven,
  Would I call you, O Muse; fairy tales help me invent!

Perhaps these lines are another proof of Mörike's homelessness in his own time. They have been interpreted in this fashion. It is possible, though, that the elegiac mood appeared to him as part of the genre of the idyl, that he imitated the themes of his ancient models.[63]

No such nostalgia is apparent in the poem "In the Vineyard," where a butterfly briefly settles on the poet's New Testament and must now carry its spirit to flowers to be picked by a girl, or in "Waldplage" (Plague in the Forest). This poem very beautifully demonstrates what humorous situations are made of: a gap between our expectations and what really happens. The difference in levels, in this case, is that of form and content. The poem is an account of an afternoon in the forest where the narrator had planned to read Klopstock's *Odes* but was too badly plagued by mosquitoes to be able to concentrate. With sarcastic humor he proceeded to kill his enemies between the pages of the book. All this he describes in the form of the trimeter to "match the two times three feet of the animals." And he addresses the hostile mosquitoes in the elevated style of the poet whose work he was reading: virgin, long-legged and, to top it off, with the most famous line of Klopstock's poem to the moon: "You flee, O stay, do not hasten, you friend of thoughts."

By contrasting the banality of the struggle with the insects with the highly poetical language, Mörike achieved not only a comical but a poeticizing effect. The same can be said about the whole group of idyllic poems, even the less humorous ones. His aim in writing them was to poeticize everyday reality. It took on a poetic shimmer, at least during his inspired moments.

The same is true of the poem "Häusliche Szene" (Domestic Scene). It is likely that experience only supplied Mörike with the character of an inventive professor, while the rest of the humorous scene sprang from his imagination. Yet it keeps us in the confines of everyday life. The poem is too long to be given here in its entirety. The following lines occur toward the end when the two combatants, the professor and his wife who is getting tired of finding jugs with vinegar everywhere, take turns discussing the use of the elegiac meter, a hexameter and a pentameter. He is the first speaker:

"I can well see you enjoy it today to spite me in verses."—
  "But what you said up to now, was it not verse just as well?"—
"If the professional has this weak side, should you try to abuse it?"—
  "Without intention, like you, I use elegiac form."—
"Only for innocent talks I taught it to you with great effort."—
  "Truly it sounds rather strange used in such serious way."—
"Therefore I cannot allow it; just speak in your everyday manner."—
  "Well, let us hear how it sounds, mixing the distich with prose."—
"Nonsense! Let us break off. It is fruitless to argue with women."—
  "Nor will your vinegar change, up in the chimney, my dear."—
"That I must have at my heels your pentameter now at the closing!"—
  "Your own hexameter draws it with magnetical force."—
"O you just wish for the chance to have the last word still, the last one:
  Have it! I swear you will not hear me another one say."—
  "For all I care! Then we let now stand this hexameter single!"—
(Pause. The man becomes restless; it obviously hurts him not to hear the distich completed or to complete it himself. After a while the woman laughingly comes to his rescue and says:)
  "Darling, I did go too far; I'll let the vinegar pass;
If in the future it turns out still better, well, then it is only
  Due to your efforts; for truly you do not have a quarrelsome wife!"—
(He also laughs heartily and kisses her:)
"Rike, tomorrow I empty for you in the front of all the windows
  And in the chimney alone make a fine sow then the hams!"

The comical effect of such dichotomy between subject matter and form was also known to other writers of the time, for example Tieck, Brentano, and Immermann.[64] They all used it for reasons of variety and playfulness. To have such a treasure of poetical forms at one's disposal was after all something rather new for German poets, whose language had only recently been enriched by an acquaintance with other literatures. It is a certain self-assurance and self-irony with regard to forms that manifests itself in such playfulness. How masterfully Mörike could handle these forms and make them seem natural in German is best shown by the longest of his Idyls, "Die Idylle vom Bodensee" ("The Idyl from Lake Constance").

The "Idyl from Lake Constance" is a sizable work (in Maync's edition it fills fifty pages) and must be compared with such works as Voss's *Luise,* in which the translator of Homer described the idyllic life of people in Northern Germany, and Goethe's *Hermann and Dorothea.*[65] Goethe tells his story against the background of the events following the French Revolution. But there are no such political implications in Mörike's work, which makes it more timeless yet also more limited. His simple country people are not linked with world history. Their tale is one of love and betrayal, of pranks and happiness. A dark figure looms in the background: Death. We hear that he will take the hero's beloved four years after the events described in the main story and long before those of the frame.

In the framing story, the hero, the fisherman Martin, is in his seventies. He is still strong and alert and ready to teach his neighbors a lesson. And thus, in 1846, Mörike made poetical use of a motif he had mentioned as early as 1828: the theft of a church bell.[66] Martin senses the greed in a tailor and his helper who talk about the bell in an old, unused chapel, and induces them to fetch it during the night. Only he knows that the bell has long since disappeared. But in order to open the tailor's eyes about his greedy behavior, he puts an old hat in the tower that looks from afar like a bell. Then while he waits for his victim, Martin remembers his youth and the prank he is most proud of. This narrative device allows us to hear of events long past which are related in the main part of the "Idyl."

Martin's friend, Tone, loved a girl, Gertrud, who was not very cheerful but harsh and greedy for money. One day she becomes jealous because Tone sings with the shepherdess Margaret. Gertrud does not see Tone for several days and then surprises him with her engagement to the simpleton son of a rich miller from another village. This arouses Martin's anger, and he plans to take revenge. On the day of her wedding, he and his friends secretly go off with the wagon that carries her dowry. In the forest they unload everything—furniture, pots, and pans—and drink and are merry until the next morning when the theft is discovered. After the newlyweds recover their possessions, the simpleton husband hungrily eats a baby made of dough he finds in the cradle, instituting thereby a saying, "He eats his own child like the miller from Baernau."

In the meantime, Tone has fully recovered from the betrayal of Gertrud. On the day of the wedding, he accidentally meets Margaret, and the two discover their love for each other. Then follows one of the most charming love scenes in German literature. Mörike begins it by invoking the good spirit of his work:

Spread out thy wings now, my song, hovering towards the fields there!
First along the light shores fly and then over the cornland
Crossing also the grass that slopes to the edge of the forest.
There, at dawn of the wedding-day, when still on the grasses
Glittered the dew and the earth breathed strengthening fragrance
Stood the loveliest girl guarding the sheep by the oaktree,
As she would sometimes do taking the place of her brother.

She stands there and looks at the sky and the distant mountains until her glance is attracted by an early wanderer: Tone, who is on his way to town. She speaks to herself and shows pity mixed with admiration for him. When he suddenly crosses the ditch and walks up to her to ask if he could shop for her in town, she declines, and then they stand silently:

Now they were silent and he, pressing close to the oaktree,
Looked from above at the girl. Then a yearning grew in his bosom,
Filled with love was his heart and excited with longing
Which had approached him before much like a delicate promise
Often when Margaret's picture had come to the mind of the lonesome
Bidding him comfort and calm and sisterly love in her gestures.
Oh, how strong was the wish in overflowing emotion
But the courage was lacking. He knew not how to begin it.

But after some preliminaries, his speech begins to flow and he tells her first of his grief over the broken engagement and how he was shaken for thirteen days and nights, until suddenly he felt free of his sorrow for Gertrud and began to look forward to the future. Slowly his attention was attracted to Margaret, whom he occasionally saw in church and on the street. He began to see her in his dreams but avoided her in the daytime, fearing she might not comprehend his sudden change of feelings. Now it had all spurted out against his will—would she think badly of him? She covers her face with her hands while he talks, but the tears she is shedding are tears of love and happiness.

The apparently simple situation may give rise to misunderstandings. Even a little more reflection on ethics might have destroyed the delicate relationship that had grown so quickly after Tone's violent feelings for another girl. Yet Mörike's characters are truly idyllic; they safely walk the narrow path where sensuality and morality are in harmony. We are reminded of Schiller for whom such harmony was the highest ideal that mankind would reach after having passed through the period of reflection. Should we understand Mörike's work as an answer to Schiller's hopes? Or is the setting in the simple life of the peasants too much like the idyls of late antiquity or of the sentimental eighteenth century that reflected a refined society's annoyance with its own conditions and its nostalgia for a simpler life? An affirmative answer would allow the conclusion that to write this story meant an escape for its author, as has often been thought. If we compare his characters, however, with those of other writers of idyls, it is amazing how much more realistically they are drawn. The "simple people" of other authors are often only dressed up in peasant costumes and do not speak and act naïvely, but are just as affected as their contemporaries in the cities. They impress us as masks. Mörike's figures, however, were possible because of the poet's own affinity to their inner nature. This was a part or a possibility of his own character, as many of his visitors felt whenever they caught him at a happy hour.

VII   *The Poetry of 1863*

Seventeen years after the publication of the "Idyl from Lake Constance" Mörike wrote "Sketches from Bebenhausen," a cycle of poems describing details of the architecture and scenes from the secular life in the former Cistercian monastery Bebenhausen, where the poet found calm and rest during some vacations in later life.[67] Among these eleven sketches of two to five distichs in length there is one, entitled, "Kunst und Natur" (Art and Nature), which points out the similarity of architectural designs with forms we find in nature. One of the short poems describes the well house in the cloister; another, in epigrammatic form, seems to laugh with Till Eulenspiegel, the mocker, whose little image supports one of the arches. The poet displays his greatest mastery in the splendid description of the chapter hall in Romanesque style and of the summer refectory, obviously of Gothic dimensions, in the poem, "Kapitelsaal":

Chapter Hall

Time after time I gaze at the hall in Romanesque splendor,
   Wonderful arches, placed stoutly on short columns' shaft.
Coarsely grained is the stone, that received the ornamentation
   Gladly, as well as the force, giving life to the weight.
Only a shadowy light the day sends in through the narrow
   Windows and here where its ray touches a long silent grave.
Rudolf the Founder and her, Mechthildis, the Pious, the convent
   Thankfully granted a place with the ordained to rest.

The next poem once more reflects Mörike's idea of beauty: the sublime is fused with a cheerful element.

Sommer-Refectorium (Summer Refectory)

One hall receives you with summer-like brightness; this is a cathedral you
   Think; but too cheerful a mood penetrates the sublime.
See, how the eye with delight now is drawn to look up at the slender
   Pillars! So lofty their build almost like that of the palm.
For from the center the ribs go out in many directions
   Up there and weave, in a curve, infinitely the net
Forming the panels for fanciful climbing blooms which the artist
   Easily painted; there lives all that roams in the woods:
Free in the air a high-jumping boar, the stag and the squirrel;
   Goshawk and pheasant and owl swing back and forth in the boughs
—When, as a guest, from the hunt the count palatine came to dine here,
   Lifting his cup he could see Paradise up there above.

The ninth poem in the cycle, "Aus dem Leben" (From Life), once more shows the master's skill in creating humor by contrasting everyday life and serious contemplation:

From Life

Girl at the wash-tub, so fair-haired, your arms you must not display here
   Nor the shoulders so bare under the abbot's old room.
He, that is true, can no longer see you. But the good forester
   There at his files you surely disturb in his peaceful work.

The last poem of the cycle, entitled, "Verzicht" (Resignation), cheerfully admits Mörike's failure to capture such art and its background in a drawing. The glittering blue sky and the warmth of the mountains were too delicate for any sketch. But he found consolation in the thought that his inner eye would retain the entire view.

Resignation is also the mood underlying another poem of the aging Mörike: "Erinna an Sappho" (Erinna to Sappho). Its central theme is death, whose presence silences joy and leaves only sadness and courage. An introductory note by Mörike explains the situation:

Erinna, a highly praised young poetess of Greek antiquity, lived around 600 B.C., friend and pupil of Sappho at Mitylene on Lesbos. She died when only nineteen. Her most famous work was an epic poem, "The Spindle," which has not come down to us. Only some fragments of a few lines and three epigrams survive. Two statues were erected for her, and the anthologies contain several epigrams written in her honor by various authors.

"There are many paths down to Hades," says an
Ancient song—"and you will have to follow one too,
Do not doubt it!" Who, my dearest Sappho, would doubt it?
Since we are told so by every day?
Yet the living do only remember lightly
Such a word, and the fisherman, close to the ocean from childhood,
Does not receive any more the roar of the waves in his ear.
Wondrously, though, today my heart was alarmed. Let me tell you!

Beautiful morning light in the garden
Flooded the tops of the trees,
Tempted the sleepy head (as you recently chided Erinna)
Early to rise from an uneasy sleep.
Peaceful appeared my mind; in my veins, however,
Restlessly throbbed my blood, yet my cheeks did look pale.

While at the dressing table I opened my tresses,
Then with the nard-scented comb on the forehead divided the veil
Of my hair,—strangely my glance was met by the glance in the mirror.
Eyes, so I said, my eyes, what do you wish for?
You, my mind, safely at home still within there,
Closely wedded to stirring senses,

How do you beckon to me with estranging earnest, half smiling,
As a demon, foretelling death!
—Ha, then at once it flashed upon me
Like lightning! as if in passing a deathly arrow,
Blackfeathered, had almost touched on my brow,
That I, while guarding my face with my hands, a long time
Kept gazing dizzily into the dark horrid cleft.

And I thought of my hour of death;
First without crying,
Until I thought of you, Sappho,
And of the other friends
And the graceful art of the Muses,
Then at once flowed my tears.

And there shone from the table the beautiful hairnet, your present.
Precious the web from byssos with golden bees swarming.
Soon, when we celebrate with gay flowers
Festively Demeter's wonderful daughter,
I would like to present it to her, in my name and yours also,
As to retain her grace (for very great is her power)
So that you may not sever too soon for Erinna
From your beloved head your curly brown hair.[68]

At first glance, the poem does not seem to follow any particular rhythmic scheme. But through the free verse the reader soon senses familiar forms, hexameters and the verses of classical odes, some of the Sapphic.[69] The rhythm itself is a perfect description of the girl who is speaking, her thoughts and her startling experience. It presents the succession of questions and answers quite naturally, yet highly artistically. Höllerer compares it to the *poésie pure* of the French poets Verlaine and Rimbaud. The content of the poem also reflects the entire range of Mörike's experiences: from playfulness almost touching on coquetry to the knowledge of the demonic, of death and an estrangement from one's self and the familiar surroundings. But there are no abstract reflections; life is transformed into images. The thought of human forgetfulness concerning daily observations, for example, is reflected in the figure of the fisherman whose ear is used to the sound of the waves. After all, it was only natural for the poetess on an island to think of the fisherman. And all the other images, too, are derived from her personal realm. This does not diminish the poem's effect on the reader: despite the unfamiliar surroundings he still feels the touch of death as if the experience were his own.

In Mörike's development as a poet, "Erinna to Sappho" occupies a similar place as the novella "Mozart on the Way to Prague." Death is the basis for everything in life, including love and poetic inspiration. Images from earlier periods of the poet's life have already prepared us for this concept. In the first Peregrina poem, the image of the hope for love's golden treasures, which lured the poet to dark caves deep in the earth, was interpreted as an invitation to death. In the sonnets of 1830, the unfathomable represented the depths of contemplation as well as the source of human destiny. We cannot help but remember these shades of the image of "depth" when Erinna looks into "the dark horrid cleft." The knowledge that death may be near intensifies her love for her friends—it is also an inspiration for poetry, as the poem itself demonstrates.

VIII *Mörike's Nonsense Poetry*

Among Mörike's writings which were not published during his lifetime, we find a few poems called "Wispeliaden." The poet pretended that they were written in 1837 by Liebmund Maria Wispel, a character who had appeared in his novel *Nolten the Painter*. Some of these verses show the comical contrast of pretentiousness and concern with the commonplace which we know from "Häusliche Szene" (Domestic Scene) and other poems. They also contain a new element: an abundance of neologisms. Whereas in his serious poetry Mörike had shown his mastery of the language by his wilful use or his peculiar combinations of well-known words—thereby calling our attention to original meanings or peculiar aspects of these expressions—he here misspells familiar words or invents completely new ones. He often uses antiquated words like *Reke* (misspelling of *Recke*) = thane, or *Zähren* (an earlier word for *Tränen*) = tears, or he adds or omits letters as in *Baigen* (for *eigen*) = peculiar, or *Uchdrucker* (for *Buchdrucker*) = printer. Important for us is the awareness of the possibility of using words independently of their meaning in contexts representative of characters and moods.

We are on the way to the Nonsense Poetry of the twentieth century—introduced into German literature by Christian Morgenstern—that combines words in a completely unconventional way, sometimes only to amuse, but in part also to indicate that all the known combinations have not yet encompassed the entire world.

Such verses are, of course, difficult to translate. The following attempt to render the few lines on the windpipe or larynx ("Der Kehlkopf") may serve as an example:

The Windpipe

The windpipe in the hollow trunk
Had pleasured us as willow-bard.
They now have come upon its bunk
And tore quite neatly up its heart.
Behind its back they had been climbing
It could not help but give up rhymbing.

Der Kehlkopf

Der Kehlkopf, der im hohlen Bom
Als Weidenschnuppe uns ergötzt
Dem kam man endlich auf das Trom,
Und hat ihn säuberlich zerbätzt,
Man kam von hinten angestiegen,
Drauf ward er vorne ausgezwiegen.

In the entire body of Mörike's poetry, the nonsense verses are not of great importance. But they point once more to his versatility and to the role of humor in his attitude toward life. This humor became more dominant in his later poems. In his prose we shall note a similar development from Romantic involvement with human nature and destiny to a playfulness above the knowledge of death.

IX *Mörike and Music*

The attentive reader of Mörike's letters will quickly notice how frequently the poet mentions the musical settings of his poetry. Several of his friends from the years at Urach and at the Tübingen Stift were able composers. They were happy to set his poems to music so that they could be sung in the art-loving circles of Swabia. Mörike himself often asked his friends Friedrich Kaufmann and Louis Hetsch, or his older brother Karl, to compose music for particular poems. Thus his brother, for example, wrote the music for two of the six songs based on poems in *Nolten the Painter* while Hetsch composed the other four. In 1838 Mörike collaborated very closely with the composer Ignaz Lachner in writing the libretto for an operetta (*Singspiel*) *Die Regenbrüder* (*The Rainbrothers*).

Mörike's text for this operetta was another fairy tale. After a long period of drought, the people of a little village are celebrating the first rain. A few of them are convinced that they owe this blessing to the three brothers, called Rainbrothers, who must have passed through the region. The enlightened schoolmaster, however, ridicules such superstition. The three mysterious brothers are said to be the sons of a powerful king and magician, Thebar, who, in an argument with his friend Alrachnod, the master of fire and wind, once made it rain so hard that the gods removed both opponents from the earth. Their children, the three sons of Thebar and the three daughters of Alrachnod, have to stay on earth and suffer for their fathers' sins. One of the girls, Justine, lives in the village at the miller's, while the other two have been banished to the nearby forest and lake and must not show themselves until two men have sworn to be faithful to them forever. Justine thus has to save them all. She employs magic to appear as one of her sisters to two of the brothers Rain; and she chooses the right one for herself. In the end, even the schoolmaster is convinced of their supernatural powers, after the brothers have forced him to fly through the air with his umbrella. This adds a comical note to the lighthearted play which has much in common with Mozart's *Magic Flute* and the plays by Mörike's Austrian contemporary Ferdinand Raimund. The opinions of the audience at the performance in Stuttgart differed. Some of Mörike's friends reported a favorable impression; others were unhappy with the composer's work.

The reaction to the settings of Mörike's poems by Kaufmann, Hetsch, and others was different. These were sung in the circles of Mörike's friends and at social gatherings, as they were best suited to intimate performances rather than the concert hall. Like Goethe, Mörike preferred the settings of his friends to those by the more famous composers of an entirely new art form:

the *Lied*. But poems like "The Forsaken Girl," or "Fair Roh-traut" were set to music by Schumann as early as 1847 and 1849; "To an Äolian Harp" and "The Sisters" by Brahms in 1858 and before 1874. Mörike's present fame is due, though, to Hugo Wolf who showed greater respect for Mörike's texts than any other composer. His compositions made Mörike known to a wider public outside of Swabia.

Hugo Wolf set to music fifty-three of Mörike's poems, many of them in one great wave of enthusiasm in 1888. According to his letters from this time, he lived in a state of frenzy and some-times composed the music for two or three poems in a day. Still, his settings are as varied as Mörike's poems themselves. He felt as if the poems were acting on him, as if inspiration came almost against his will.[70] He completely subjected himself and his music to the poetry and showed such fine understanding of each of the poems that he became Mörike's best interpreter, a far better one than most literary historians of his time, who still described Mörike as the Swabian country parson with a very limited ho-rizon. Hugo Wolf's settings reveal the depth of Mörike's poetry; they show the demonic powers hidden in it and let his audi-ences partake in the experiences of joy and bitterness, of awe and humor. As Wolf's songs were accepted by ever growing audi-ences, people also became aware of the wealth and melodiousness of Mörike's poetry.[71]

Melodiousness is, indeed, inherent in the poetry itself. In the discussions of the poetry above we have noted how important the rhythm is in Mörike's poems, and we have seen that at times the sound of the words, in conjunction with rhythm and rhyme, ex-press the meaning of the poem without the help of the literal sense of the words. Rhythm above all seems to be the quality that distinguishes poetry from prose[72]—it makes poetry analo-gous to music, which also depends on rhythm. But Mörike's poems have melodious elements besides the rhythm; namely, rhyme, assonance, onomatopoeia, and alliteration. He used rhyme even in his free rhythm. The effect of rhyming, that is, of returning to a sound still ringing in the listener's ear, resembles that of melody. Vowels are most important, since, even their repetition, as in assonance, brings about a musical effect. But also the frequent use of some consonants, *l*, *r*, *m*, and *n*, creates

rhythm. Alliteration does the same. Mörike used all these devices with great sophistication. This becomes clear in his defense
of the use of imperfect rhymes in his edition of Waiblinger's poetry. Such discords are more subtle than perfect rhymes and
challenge particularly the modern composer. His contemporaries, who were strongly interested in folk songs since the Romanticists had celebrated them in their collections, were also inspired
by Mörike's use of the refrain in his folk song-like poems.

No wonder, then, that Mörike's poetry found so many composers. More than three hundred composers have been listed;
they wrote close to six hundred compositions of as many as 123
Mörike poems.[73] The poems most frequently set to music are
"The Forsaken Girl," "An Hour before the Day," "Er ist's" (It Is
Spring) and "Fair Rohtraut." To this very day recitals which
feature the German *Lied* are therefore likely to include a few
songs with texts by Eduard Mörike.

CHAPTER 3

Mörike's Prose

I *The Artist's Calling and Life;* Nolten the Painter *and "Mozart on the Way to Prague"*

FOR a short time in the history of German literature it appeared as if Goethe's novel *Wilhelm Meisters Lehrjahre* (*Wilhelm Meister's Apprenticeship*), which was published in 1795-96, had given final shape to what the Germans call *Entwicklungsroman* or *Bildungsroman,* a novel of education that describes the development of the protagonist as in Fielding's *Tom Jones,* or a work with even stronger emphasis on intellectual growth and, often, a deeper understanding of artistic creation. But the Romantics, first enthusiastic about Goethe's work, soon attempted to improve upon it. They criticized Wilhelm Meister's turning away from the arts to a practical life among an aristocracy that was concerned with the improvement of agriculture, crafts, and welfare. Instead of portraying the individual's entry into society, they stressed the freedom of the individual, especially the artist, from society. The gap between artist and society became a tragic experience in the works of E. T. A. Hoffmann and in Eduard Mörike's first novel, *Nolten the Painter.*

In their discussions of Mörike's novel, many critics pay little attention to the fact that the protagonist is an artist. This attitude has a certain justification because Nolten never demands any particular privileges as an artist or exhibits any eccentricities. He rather gives the impression of a sensitive young man who has a fine understanding of various styles of art—the classical and the romantic—and would be most happy if he could live as a productive member of society—except that he would like to create works of art instead of articles for practical use. But there is one strain in him which does not allow him to settle down. This part of his character is symbolized by the inextricable connection between him and the fatal personage of the novel: the "gypsy" Elisabeth. Her kinship with Nolten is explained only at the end of the novel, although the reader divines it from the moment he hears of her resemblance to a painting found in the house of Nolten's parents. It is from the first meeting of the sixteen-year-old boy with this beautiful and mysterious girl that Nolten's artistic calling dates. We find the description of this encounter almost halfway through the novel in an interpolation entitled :"A Day from Nolten's Youth." Beck reads this inserted piece as a *Künstlerberufungsnovelle,* a novella in which an artist begins to realize his calling.[1]

The inserted story begins on a gloomy day in late October when Nolten and his sister Adelheid decide to go on an excursion to some ruins on a hill in the forest two hours away from home. The gray and melancholy day fills them with joy—creating one of those mixed moods Mörike so often described in his poetry. When they reach their destination, they separate without noticing it, because their attention is drawn to different points of interest. Suddenly Adelheid hears the voice of a woman singing a melancholy tune not unlike those issuing from an Äolian harp. A moment later Nolten runs up to his sister, telling her of a woman whom he has seen from a distance. They decide to look for her, in order to help in case she has lost her way or is in trouble. They find a foreign-looking girl who resembles a gypsy. Her beautiful face and figure instill awe and confidence in them (Peregrina!). She has a mysterious effect on Nolten. He turns pale, begins to tremble, and faints. Adelheid becomes very excited, but the stranger begs her to be quiet and with a hypnotic gesture puts her hand on the boy's forehead and whispers to him. He opens his eyes—Adelheid runs for their provisions—and Nolten begins to talk. He tries to explain to the stranger what has happened to him:

When I looked at you, I felt as if I were sinking deep down into myself as into an abyss, as if I were staggering, plunging from depth to depth, through all the nights where I have seen you in a thousand dreams, like this, as you stand there before me; I whirled around through all the periods of my life and saw myself as a boy and saw myself as a child next to your figure as it is now raised before me again! Indeed, I came to the darkness where my cradle stood and I saw you hold the veil that covered me: then I lost consciousness, I may have slept for a long time, but when my eyes were opened as by their own will, I looked into yours as into an infinite well, wherein lay the mystery of my life.[2]

Nolten's impassioned remarks remind us of Ludwig Bauer's description of the impression that Maria Meyer had made on Mörike. And when we consider the important role which such images as that of the abyss and the well play in Mörike's poetry, we cannot doubt that these lines touch on the central experience of Nolten the Painter. From this moment on, Nolten's artistic gift will be insuppressible. He is destined for a secret union with Elisabeth, the mysterious girl, which he will try to repudiate later, as he seeks the love of other women. His efforts will fail because their union has also become an obsession with Elisabeth. She will find him wherever he goes and will disturb his other relationships. Not that she will show herself to him—no, without his knowledge she will approach the other women and confuse their feelings, for they are all hypersensitive.

The sensitivity of the characters is another important aspect of the novel. Mörike's concern with the psychology of the main figures is extraordinary for a novel written in 1830. From the very beginning of the story, Mörike motivates his characters on two different levels. The first level is that of destiny which seems to rule man's fate so that he must either feel powerless or simply accept it as an expression of his own will (this idea of freedom as a result of conscious acceptance of fate may have been influenced by Schiller). Nolten expresses it at a later stage of the novel:

"I am happy that, while a divine power is guiding me, I am actually only aware of *my own* will, of *my own* thoughts. Man steers his carriage wherever it pleases him, but below the globe on which he rides unnoticeably revolves. . ."[3]

The idea that man must accept his destiny helplessly had been elaborated on by some Romantics in their so-called dramas of destiny. From a modern point of view, it can be explained as an indication that man at that point in intellectual history experienced not only the Romantic's faith in the central role of the Self but also the complete reversal of this faith, a feeling of impotence in the face of the powers outside the Self.

On the other level of motivation, Mörike's attempts to find a psychological explanation for the individual's actions and experiences can also be traced back to the Romantics and their concern with the Self. Mörike's novel was a valuable contribution to the development of such understanding.[4]

In Elisabeth, for example, the poet drew a character out of contact with normal surroundings, wandering aimlessly except for one fixed goal: the attachment to Nolten after this first encounter. Adelheid at once recognizes that the girl's mind is deranged when she notices Elisabeth's strange behavior after Nolten's disclosure. Again the wandering girl had begun to sing incomprehensible words. And Nolten has to appeal to his sister's love for himself to make her take the girl home.

Once they arrive home, we witness an astounding scene. The children's father also turns pale upon seeing her—he realizes that she is his brother's daughter from a marriage the family had not approved of. The brother was a painter and on one of his trips had fallen in love with a gypsy and married her, but she died in childbirth having been sick with longing for the freedom of the woods. He had disappeared, leaving behind a painting of his wife. Without his father's knowledge young Nolten had long ago discovered this picture in the attic.

Elisabeth obviously could not know her relatives; she had been stolen by the gypsies when she was six and had later escaped from them. She is not willing now to stay in the Noltens' well-ordered home either. She walks away after supper, leaving behind a distraught Nolten, who can only hope to find her again some day, and a relieved father, who will tell Adelheid and her older sister the story of his brother after the other children are in bed. As he tells the story, we can sense his fear that young Nolten may have inherited too many traits from his uncle. For this reason he does not want his son to become a painter.

By another familiar device of the novelists of the time, the reader is acquainted with the uncle's story through a second interpolation, the painter's diary. There is no room for it in our summary; though it may be interesting to remark that it gives us the background for the character of Elisabeth, who may have been modeled after Goethe's Mignon, the wandering, unhappy girl in *Wilhelm Meister*.[5] The interpolation of the day in Nolten's youth and the uncle's diary thus make us more deeply aware of the fact that we are dealing with men of exceptional mentality, that of artists; and the two literary devices will help us to understand their actions in the earlier parts of the novel.

To return to the beginning: the novel really starts with some confusion that has been caused by Wispel. This ever changing character, whose highest ambition it is to be a confidence man and to pose as an artist or scholar has betrayed Nolten, who is now living in the capital of a German principality. (After the death of his father, he had first stayed in the house of a forester that will be the scene of many important developments in the novel.) In the city where he wanted to further his education as a painter, Nolten had hired Wispel to be his valet. Not satisfied with such an inferior role, Wispel stole some of Nolten's drafts, took them to another painter, Tillsen, and pretended that they were his own. In order to impress his alleged colleague, he intersperses flashes of ingenuity with their conversation, such as one would not expect among his otherwise nonsensical chatter. Tillsen concludes that he is insane. But his own creativity has been at an ebb for months, and he buys the drafts and executes them in a masterful manner. One oil painting and several watercolors arouse the interest and admiration of art lovers. Their recognition of the paintings embarrasses Tillsen, who was not planning to deck himself with borrowed plumes. He is relieved when Nolten comes to him and explains what has happened.

This meeting of the two artists marks the beginning of a friendship. For Nolten, the meeting is important because it results in his self-realization as an artist. He also learns techniques which he had not been able to master before. He becomes the favorite of a circle of aristocrats. The fusion in his art of a bizarre imagination with a striving for grace appeals to them.[6] One of Nolten's sketches has a bearing on the events in the novel and may therefore serve as an example. The sketch exhibits a nocturnal assembly of deceased individuals. Their faces and figures are not gruesome, however, but only pale and dressed in gray. They have gathered for a concert on a meadow in the forest not far from a chapel and, probably, close to the cemetery. Among the many figures, the girl at the organ is most attractive. Her black eyes are full of deep feeling and hardly pay attention to her surroundings. She is lost in thought and seems "to contemplate the possibility of leaving this second life, too." Next to her, a sleepy youth leans against the organ. He holds a burning torch; and a golden brown moth sits in his hair. For the reader who is acquainted with German literature, the youth calls to mind the discussions of the respective value of Pagan and Christian thoughts and symbols. Lessing, for example, had preferred to think of Death as the ancients had done. The figure of a youth with an extinguished torch appealed more to him than the Christian skeleton. The moth in the youth's hair reminds us that the butterfly in Mörike's poetry is a symbol of the soul.

The extent to which Mörike was concerned with fusing the spirit of antiquity with that of Christianity—like Goethe, Schiller, Hölderlin, and many Romantics before him—is obvious also in a conversation between Nolten and his friend, the actor Larkens, which Larkens recalls later in the novel: "We were discussing, as you know, the relationship of the deeply religious and especially Christian-minded artist to the spirit of antiquity and the poetic perception of the ancients, the possibility of an almost equally careful cultivation of both tendencies in one person. I credited you with great and rare universality, and I am sure *everybody* must agree with me."[7]

This conversation takes place at a critical point of the novel. Nolten's acceptance by the aristocratic circle has led him to believe that he would be able to win the love of Countess Constanze, the real center of the gatherings. She has indicated a lively interest in his art, and he admires her charm because it lacks the affectation so often found in persons of her station. He gladly forgets his older ties to Agnes, the daughter of the forester who had been a second father to him. His friend Larkens, however, watches the development with alarm. He is convinced that it will be harmful to Nolten's creativeness. Nolten's art, so he feels, would flourish better in the modest calm and simplicity of a limited country existence than in the distracting and demanding atmosphere of high society. To prove his point, Larkens reproaches his friend for not having spent much time at his work recently—

to no avail. Nolten is too deeply involved already, as the following scene indicates:

On a beautiful winter morning, Nolten decides to accept an invitation by the Countess' brother to one of the royal castles in the neighborhood of the city. He is riding on horseback, and the wonderful day, as well as his hope of finding the Countess at the castle, fill him with joy and expectation, which he expresses in a song that Mörike inserts in the novel. Many of his readers took Mörike's frequently lyrical interpolations as a mark of the Romantic influence on the work, others criticized the poet for using his prose as a vehicle for his basically lyric gifts. Both attitudes overlook the value these songs have as expressions of the fleeting or deep-seated sentiments in the hearts of the characters. Nolten's song, for example, expresses his feelings at this moment: his eagerness to do great deeds, to prove his courage, and to win his beloved's favor. The song thus serves as a prologue to his conversation with Constanze a short time later, in which he indicates restlessness and dissatisfaction with his achievements. Using the same arguments as Larkens, he describes how the wish to contribute to the entertainments of society keeps him from concentrating on his own work. His intention is to let her feel that he wishes for a change in his situation. She answers somewhat reprimandingly and thereby renews his uncertainty—just at the moment when their path leads into a dark grotto. Here she becomes uncertain of the way and holds on to him for protection. The tension grows when they hear the nearby footsteps of the duke, whom Nolten considers his rival. He loses control of himself and stammers words of love while holding Constanze in his arms. But only for a short moment—then she pulls herself away, leaving him in doubt about her feelings. But even this is more than he had dared to hope for in the morning. Since she has not rejected him, he convinces himself that his wish is nearing fulfillment and that Constanze will be his. This is, indeed, a critical point in his career, if Larkens is right.

Nolten does not apprise his friend of his new hopes, but Larkens can sense that he must do something decisive if he wants to prevent Nolten from sacrificing his art for his love. His secret plan is carried out two weeks later after an evening's entertainment in the house of the Count. It will have more severe consequences for Nolten and for Larkens himself than he could have anticipated because of the reaction of the audience that evening. Mörike inserts another interpolation, the shadow play "Orplid," which Larkens and Nolten present to the circle.[8] The Countess herself and a number of other guests are truly delighted with this little masterpiece, the product of Larkens' colorful imagination. Other members of the audience, however, begin to whisper. They sense in the play a disrespectful hint at the relationship of the late king with a much younger lady. It is an open secret that the king had vainly tried to escape this union as he was getting older—just as King Ulmon in the play would like to free himself from the magic spell of the fairy Thereile. The anger of this part of the audience influences Constanze when her confidence in Nolten is shaken later that night through Larkens' interference.

Larkins' plan goes into effect after the show. The guests have left and Constanze is unable to sleep. She goes to the room of her maid for a chat and finds the girl frantically hiding some papers she has been reading. This arouses Constanze's curiosity. She reaches for the papers and discovers that they are letters addressed to Nolten by an unknown girl. The maid confesses that she has found them behind the box with the pictures for the shadow play. Constanze takes the letters from the girl and—as Larkens had hoped—cannot resist the temptation to read them. She finds the expressions of Agnes' innocent faith in Nolten and must take him for a scoundrel who had deceived them both when he was giving them signs of affection at the same time; for the letters had been written recently. Constanze cannot help but feel that Nolten has not been honest with her.

The true story of these letters is most precarious. They were really answers to letters which Larkens had written in Nolten's handwriting. For when he had noticed, months earlier, that Nolten was no longer writing to Agnes, the forester's daughter, Larkens had continued the correspondence for him. He was convinced that, in time, Nolten would be thankful if Agnes' tender love was preserved for him. He asked Agnes to mail her letters to an address where he could easily intercept them. Nolten, meanwhile, lived assured that his earlier ties had been dissolved without complications. No doubt, it was a highly unconventional

measure that Larkens chose to serve his friend. In order to understand him, a brief account of his character and development
is necessary.

Larkens is a very modern figure, one of the *Zerrissenen* (torn
between opposites), as this type of person was labelled in a contemporary novel. Mörike refused to read the novel because
he could not respect people who were not striving for inner
harmony.[9] We know, however, that he felt this tendency in his
own character. Whatever has been said about Mörike's attempts
to hide behind masks, about his proximity to the experience of
ennui and his forlornness in the stream of time, holds true
for the figure of Larkens. He is a great actor because he can
change his identity completely and gladly, can become a different
person with that person's feelings, language, and features. When
he is not acting, he feels bored and dissatisfied with himself. He
therefore derives a sense of fulfillment as he is playing Nolten's
role, not only because he is convinced that he is doing his friend
a service, but also because he begins to feel the virtue of the love
he is simulating in the letters to Agnes. He is almost sorry when
the end of his role approaches. But he has set the date for this
end himself. He will present Nolten with his gift of an unscathed
love at the moment when Nolten's affection for Constanze is
brought to end. But Nolten's and Constanze's suffering at that moment and the ensuing developments will by far surpass Larkens'
expectations.

For Constanze, having read Agnes' letters, in a weak moment
gives way to the longing for revenge because her pride is hurt.
Asked by the duke whether she considers the friends guilty of *lèse
majesté*, she joins the group of accusers, and the friends are im-
prisoned. This change from bliss to misery, caused by Constanze's
betrayal, as he must see it, are too much for Nolten. He contracts
a nervous fever, and Larkens must admit to himself that his plans
are getting out of hand. The situation appears to be hopelessly
entangled.

But the author comes to Nolten's help and shows a new way
out of the labyrinth of emotions and misunderstandings. In Nolten's feverish fantasies, the picture of Agnes begins to replace that
of Constanze. The lovely, uncomplicated girl seems to offer rest
and consolation to his tortured mind. This impression is intensi-

fied by the effect of a folk song he hears through the window, the song about a forsaken girl. Only now does he realize his own guilt toward Agnes. In the eyes of the readers, this guilt has long been mitigated through reports about a nervous condition of the girl, of which Nolten either did not know or had heard only in distorted form. Nolten was thus justified, to a certain degree, in doubting her loyalty.

If we sum up the information we receive about Agnes in various parts of the novel, we are faced with the surprisingly precise pathography of a neurosis. At age ten Agnes had already shown the first signs of monomania. She was convinced that all adults were taking part in a plot against her; that, wherever she went, people talked intentionally about things which did not really exist, simply to excite her imagination. She outgrew this idea, however, and when Nolten meets her, her character appears calm and harmonious and at one with reality. He does not notice that she sometimes wonders whether she is really the person he needs because of her lack of education. During Nolten's absence, she becomes seriously ill with a nervous fever. She recovers but retains an irritability that others cannot understand. They do not know that shortly after her sickness, after accompanying her cousin Otto a little way to the city, she has received a severe shock. She meets a gypsy who offers to tell her fortune and predicts that she would not marry the sweetheart she was thinking of but the cousin she had just bade farewell. Agnes promises not to tell anybody of this encounter and thus is entirely alone with the horrible notion that she has lost what was dearest to her: her relationship to Nolten.

The fact that Agnes has her own doubts about the future of their love makes her an easy prey for Elisabeth, whom the reader, of course, recognizes as the gypsy. Whether Elisabeth herself believes what she tells Agnes or whether she poisons the girl intentionally, we will never know. It is certain, however, that she also interferes with Nolten's relationship with Countess Constanze. Constanze has been so deeply impressed by the organist in Nolten's painting that she sees this figure in a dream saying, "Constanze Josephine Armond will soon play the organ with us, too." At the time of Nolten's imprisonment when she is tormented by remorse because she has betrayed him, Constanze one day dis-

covers the model for the painting, Elisabeth, in church. She believes that she is seeing an apparition announcing her imminent
death. From then on, we see Constanze ailing. Elisabeth thus
plays a fatal role in the life of both women. And Larkens and
Nolten, when they independently discover these intertwinements,
can only feel that the past, in the person of Elisabeth, is forever
threatening Nolten's present.[10]

Elizabeth's interference causes a most pitiful confusion in
Agnes' feelings. She is torn between hope and resignation and
even resentment against Nolten. To surprise her beloved with a
new talent, she decides to take lessons in mandolin playing from
her cousin Otto. But that creates further difficulties. Mindful of
the gypsy's prophesy, she alternates between antipathy toward
him and playful flirtation. Her flirtation is reported to Nolten
by a well-meaning friend and also by Otto himself, who asks him
to relinquish his claims to the girl. A letter from Agnes' father,
who is enraged by Otto's action, follows. But Nolten is not com-
forted and is unhappy over Agnes' behavior. This is the moment
when Larkens takes over the correspondence.

In the meantime, the father, suspecting a sort of insanity in
his daughter, has called a physician, who finally detects the secret
source of the disturbance: the influence of Elisabeth. At the moment when she discloses her secret, Agnes begins to recover; her
love for Nolten blossoms again and gives charm to the letters of
which Larkens is the receiver. At this point, Larkens decides to
return Agnes to Nolten, who has recovered from his illness. To
make it impossible for Nolten to reject his efforts and the girl's
love, Larkens himself leaves town for an undefined period of
time, placing the entire correspondence on his desk where Nolten
must find it.

Nolten is deeply moved by losing his friend and regaining
Agnes at the same time. The knowledge that Agnes' delicate
mind has suffered so much because of him and the mysterious
figure of Elisabeth fills him with overflowing pity and love. He
saddles his horse and sets out on the journey. Some literary historians interpret this journey back to the place of his childhood
as the reversal of the *Bildungsroman* (novel of education), since
Nolten returns to his point of departure. "The hero cannot ad-
vance, in the sense that Wilhelm Meister advances, because he

cannot shake off his own past."[11] He is going back to Agnes and her small idyllic world; and as he ultimately loses her, he will even be pulled back into the dark world of Elisabeth.

The reader may stop here and think of Mörike's personal situation at the time of the conception of the novel. The work was published in 1832 during the time of Mörike's love for Luise Rau. By 1828 the poet had re-evaluated his experience with Maria Meyer, as we have seen in our discussion of the Peregrina poems. If we can believe the novel, the knowledge of his guilt still burdens him and threatens his new love for Luise. Maria Meyer was not likely to interfere in person, like Elisabeth in the novel, but Mörike knew only too well that his range of experience was wider than that of Luise. And she may have sensed this too. Some biographers tell us that Luise Rau resented the reflection of her character in the novel. Unable to comprehend the poet's right to fuse traits of real characters with the creatures of his imagination, she could only feel that some of her characteristics were exaggerated in the image of Agnes, who was obviously modeled after her. We do not know how much this resentment contributed to terminating the engagement.

Critics have compared Mörike's relationship to his *Nolten the Painter* with that of Goethe to his novel *Werther* and have stated that Mörike succumbed as little to the dark forces which bring about Nolten's end as Goethe died the death of his Werther.[12] This comparison is correct only if we think of a larger span of Mörike's lifetime and his poetic achievements. At the time when the novel was finished, the mysteriousness in the poet's character still made Luise shy away from him.

This glance at the novel as a whole and its tragic outcome should not smother the reader's enjoyment of the part that follows Nolten's departure from the city. This, too, was written during the time of Mörike's engagement, but it reflects happiness and fulfillment just like the poet's letters to Luise. As many critics have seen, Mörike was not a great master at painting the picture of the life of aristocrats or Bohemians, but he is unsurpassed in his description of the idyllic country life around Agnes' home. The scene, for example, in which Nolten, upon his arrival, observes Agnes who sits with her knitting on the wall of the blooming cemetery and watches a butterfly or talks to a stork, has often been quoted. And the first moments of stammering happiness after she discovers the hidden observer, or the cozy family scene in the evening when Nolten is asked by the forester to give an account of his life in the city, are genre pieces for which Mörike could draw from his own rich personal experience.

The following days of Nolten's stay in the forester's house are filled with small scenes which often create mixed feelings in Nolten, who is reminded of his betrayal and of Agnes' past afflictions. These psychologically difficult situations provide the author with opportunities for many fine observations. Thus, Nolten may suddenly reproach himself for being so happy while his friend Larkens is wandering over the face of the earth without friendship and help. At other times, Nolten feels left out of the happy union of father and daughter. It seems to him that they had never meant anything to him. In another scene, Agnes' father reminds her of the mandolin playing. The effect of this observation on the girl is most frightening: "The beautiful girl flushed to a dark red at this word. Her eyes became suddenly moist without shedding tears and opened very wide, as can be observed in somnambulists. It was impossible then to look at her, for one became intensively afraid she would dissolve like a miracle, melt completely like a light cloud."[13]

Such scenes and observations, and the reminiscences of their happy days before Nolten's stay in the city, are so numerous in the novel that the concept of the *Künstlerroman* (novel of an artist) is hardly preserved. An excursion that leads them into the neighboring hills on a visit seems to be contrived only to introduce the legend of Volker (whom we met before in Mörike's mythical poetry), the brave and cheerful leader of a band of robbers who had given up his unfettered life in these hills to atone for the killing of a white stag.

But during this visit, Mörike reintroduces the theme of Nolten's development as an artist. Another artist, the sculptor Raymund, meets them and hands Nolten a letter inviting him to the court of a north-German prince. Both Raymund and Nolten are offered a lifetime appointment by the art-loving ruler. Nolten can hardly believe his good fortune, which is announced in the letter by a distant acquaintance of his and a protector of Raymund, an old court councillor whose interest in his destiny Nolten cannot understand. He considers the offer of such an honorable position as a challenge and the possible climax of his career as an artist. Nolten begins to look forward to reaching this peaceful harbor after his wanderings.

This elation is of short duration. When they return to the village, Agnes and Nolten find an old friend dying. On the following days, Agnes behaves very strangely. She finally admits that she is obsessed by the fear of a much greater misfortune. When they discuss a wedding date, she begs to postpone it at least for a month, but without being able to give a logical reason. Her father loses his temper over her obstinacy, and Nolten begins to wonder how they can ever be happy. He is certain, though, that he loves her more than ever before and, knowing that her troubles all stem from the same source as his own fate, he resolves to accept whatever good or evil the future may bring in union with her. Yet from this time on a presentiment of doom hovers over the couple.

A few weeks later, Agnes and Nolten, accompanied by his youngest sister Nannette, start out on a journey to various places in Germany which Nolten had long wanted to see. They come to a former imperial town (Mörike avoids all place names and precise dates) where the author asks his readers—in one of his many remarks addressed to them—to leave the travelers in the best inn and to follow their coachman to a tavern for the common people instead.

In the tavern, attention is focused on a group of regular customers and especially on one person, a man of thirty-six with a noble figure, furrowed face, and fiery eyes, called Joseph the Carpenter. He is treated with particular respect by his companions, and the reader suspects that he is hiding his real identity. His true name will be given away by Wispel, who has also just arrived in town. Wispel is being angrily discussed by the group trying to find out his newest tricks. When Wispel comes to the tavern and recognizes Nolten's coachman, he is quick to run to his former master to tell him about Joseph/Larkens, although he has received money from Larkens to preserve his secret. Nolten hurries to the tavern but does not dare speak to his friend, whose disguise depresses him. He leans against a pillar, his eyes filled with tears, because he cannot understand why Larkens has to demean himself so much. At this moment, Larkens looks up, recognizes Nolten, and rushes out through a side door. Nolten and Wispel are unable to follow him, and Nolten returns to the inn, where he spends a sleepless night. The next morning Wispel bursts into his room speechless with horror and sorrow: Larkens has taken his life. What could have been more painful to Nolten, who must feel that his appearance had hastened this unfortunate decision!

There is no room here to relate Nolten's grief and his encounters with Larkens' recent companions. Only one encounter is of importance, that with President von K., who introduces himself as an admirer of Larkens. A few months before, he had recognized the actor by chance among the audience at a performance of Ludwig Tieck's *Verkehrte Welt* (The World Turned Topsy-Turvy). He now endears himself to Nolten through a few penetrating remarks about Larkens' character and art. Once more the reader gains the impression that Nolten is not the only hero of the novel, and that Mörike's reflections on art and artists are allotted to Nolten and Larkens alike. Larkens was most successful in the role of comical characters, a fact which causes the president to observe:

"Even your friend's admirable talent which delighted the world was not as harmless as it seemed; if the flame of the serene mind fed painfully on the best oil of the inner being, who tells me why such unspeakable pain—which at times undermines all manliness, all mirth and strength of the soul by softening it fearfully, at other times forces the soul beyond its bounds in anger—why such homelessness of the mind, such longing for the distance and for nowhere amidst a rich and beautiful existence is so often the legacy of excellent characters."[14]

In Mörike's poems, the reader would look in vain for a similar confession concerning the effort which the creative process requires. In his poems as well as in his letters, Mörike attempted to present the image of a poet who received his inspiration as a gift showered upon him from heaven that required little exertion on his part. Only the figure of Larkens, that of Mozart in "Mozart on the Way to Prague," and our knowledge of Mörike's personal life give us the right to have our doubts of the image Mörike created and to suspect that he also knew moments when his creativeness seemed to feed "on the best oil of his inner being."

The president invites Nolten, Agnes, and Nannette to visit him on his estate for a few days of seclusion where they might honor Larkens' memory together. Nolten accepts, and an entirely new world opens up. The life of the landed aristocracy must have been a wish-dream for our poet. More than to the society in the city he attributed to the gentry in the country a sensitivity for cultural values which comes close to the creativity of the artist himself. In "Mozart on the Way to Prague" he once more pictured the life on such a country estate. Historically, such an existence had been possible during the Rococo period, in the late eighteenth century before industrialization took place. In Mörike's time, this atmosphere still lingered on in some of the German courts, and it is no accident that Nolten's call comes from the ruler at "W.," which the German reader must be tempted to complete as Weimar, the court at which Wieland, Goethe, Herder, and Schiller had been welcome. The reality of an artist's life at court was not always ideal, but it involved a certain recognition that acted as a stimulus for his ambition.

For Nolten, the understanding which the president and his educated and independent daughter, Margot, show him, is also comforting. Margot, a more austere forerunner of Eugenie in "Mozart on the Way to Prague," becomes very friendly with Agnes. She impresses everybody with her versatility. They are fascinated by her melodious reading of Italian poetry and astounded by her strong interest in geography, which is reflected in a globe she has made. Music also plays a role in their cultural endeavors. It is a living element on the estate in the person of the blind son of the gardener, who plays his own fantasies and copies Margot's play on the piano and on the organ. Besides, they all attend a performance of Handel's *Messiah* in the city.

The days of contemplation and comfort come to a sudden end after Nolten spends a few hours in a labyrinth in the garden with the notes and letters which Larkens had bequeathed to him.[15] Among these papers, Nolten finds several poems by Larkens— numbers one, two, three, and five of the Peregrina cycle. Of course, he must recognize his own relationship to Elisabeth even through the fantastic form Larkens has given it. The magic of this vision acts like an intoxicating poison on Nolten's soul, and he remains melancholic that day even in the presence of Agnes, and even while they are watching a thunderstorm from which they hide under the roof of a belvedere. Agnes seeks to sympathize with him and mentions Larkens' name. Her remark opens Nolten's soul; he cannot keep his secret any longer and blurts out the story of Larkens' letters to Agnes. In doing this, he overestimates her calmness and self-assurance and the fortitude of their love. Agnes becomes frighteningly silent; he tries to stop his confession but has said too much already. It is too late: Agnes again loses her mental balance, now that she has lost the conviction of his loyalty. She withdraws from him and everyone else, and during the next days her affliction becomes more and more serious. She no longer recognizes Nolten, confusing him with Larkens, whom she now considers her true lover for whom she must wait while the traitor Nolten tries to interfere with their real love. Her condition becomes hopeless after another meeting with Elisabeth. The gypsy lets her know that Nolten had long promised her his love. Thus, he must have been faithless to them both when he courted Constanze.

Nolten reacts with despair and anger and curses his fate. He accuses heaven and pulls his hair and then becomes unnaturally quiet, as if the pain had numbed him. The president is moved by the tragic involvement and tries in vain to help overcome Agnes' resentment of Nolten. They advise Nolten to leave for a while in order not to disturb her. Agnes lingers on, spending most of her time with the blind son of the gardener, with Larkens' gifts, and with some poetry by Larkens which she found among his notes and letters.

These are the poems we have discussed in connection with Luise Rau and the poem "During Passion Week," all verses which express a tender faithful love that Agnes would have liked to experience. One morning they find her bed untouched; she has escaped—hopefully to go home to her father. This hope is false; they find her dead in a well that had played a role in a legend of a true and faithful love. Nolten returns, aged and burned out by his sorrow. Agnes is buried, and on the night of her funeral Nolten is awakened by the sound of the organ. He arouses the gardener and his son, but they cannot hear anything. Only after Nolten has left them and is approaching the old chapel do the sounds become audible to them; at the same time, they hear a scream and a loud noise as from a fall. They find Nolten dead in front of the chapel; but when they want to hurry to him, the boy exclaims: "By God, I can see! There—over there, he also stands and someone else with him—now they approach us—horror—O flee—" and he faints.

With this terror episode the novel draws to a close. There is still a last unveiling of secrets with a letter from the old gentleman who had helped Nolten and Raymund procure the position at "W." He is the uncle long believed dead, the painter, and the father of Elisabeth; and he is longing to disclose his identity to his nephew. It is too late—also for Elisabeth. A few days before Nolten she has died from exhaustion in the vicinity of the estate.

Elisabeth's apparition at the end of the novel, which is visible only to Nolten and the blind boy, is no unexpected miracle for Mörike readers. Among the poet's occasional writings there are several that are concerned with supernatural phenomena. One fragment, entitled "Doppelte Seelentätigkeit" (Double Action of the Soul) by the editor Maync, was never published, but the two short reports "Aus dem Gebiete der Seelenkunde" (From the Field of Psychology) appeared in the periodical *Freya* in 1861 and a longer one about "Der Spuk im Pfarrhause zu Cleversulzbach" (The Spook in the Parsonage at Cleversulzbach) was published in Kerner's *Magicon* in 1842. The latter is a description of various noises like knocking, groaning, pistol shots, of sensations as from the touch of a hand, and of visual phenomena of certain light effects experienced by several people during their stay in the parsonage. Mörike collected their reports upon the wish of his friend, the Swabian Romantic Justinus Kerner, who published the *Magicon* for items of this kind. Mörike himself did not know what to make of these experiences. It seems as if he did not want to get too deeply involved with a belief in spirits and yet could not quite deny that such phenomena existed. He tried to explain some of them by "the double action of the soul." He felt that the human soul is as active when a person is asleep as when he is awake. In the night sphere it perceives things unknown to him in the day. It might be, however, that the notions and images of the day and night spheres alternate so quickly that the night sphere could influence a conscious person without his realizing it.

The value or correctness of this explanation is not as relevant to us as the fact that such considerations should warn us against a misinterpretation of Nolten's death. Elisabeth's role is not to embody the unreal—even in his fairy tales Mörike will remain closer to the realm of reality than most other authors—but the irrational, those elements of the human soul and fate for which we have not yet found an explanation.

The circumstances of Nolten's death once more remind us of the various elements of the novel as a whole. The influence of the irrational and the occult can be explained on two levels: the psychological, as we have seen in Mörike's own attempts at understanding such phenomena, and on the level of demonic fate which rules man's life with or without his own will. At one point in the novel, Mörike widens the prospect of the influence of fate beyond Nolten's life and establishes a relationship between Nolten's fate and that of his uncle by saying that Nolten had to bring to an end the unfinished role of his ancestor whom he resembled so much in his gifts and experiences.[16] The horror that is inherent in such an idea of predestination and in its actual execution at the end of the novel, when the demonic power in the figure of Elisabeth receives Nolten even in the world beyond the earthly realm, may remind the reader of the shudders he experienced upon reading the "dramas of destiny" of the Romantics. It also points ahead in the literary development toward the modern drama, which shows man at the boundaries of existence.

The fact that Mörike chose an artist to demonstrate such extreme human experience also places him in the midst of a literary development. The Romantics, like Novalis, had first seen the artist as a human being who exemplified human possibilities more intensely than any other type of person; in their opinion he was closer to the sources of life, a prophet who could explain life's mysteries to his fellow man. In the novels of Thomas Mann the artist more than any other person experiences the deathly danger of involvement with demonic forces and man's ultimate forlornness. The question whether Nolten's fate was an unavoidable result of his being an artist must remain unanswered. No doubt, Elisabeth embodies his fate as well as his artistic calling.

Would he have found a less tragic end if he had remained loyal to her and had not searched for personal happiness, first in society, and then in the quiet life with Agnes?[17] Had Larkens been wrong in hoping that his friend could be more fortunate than he and combine creativity with such quiet happiness? There are no simple answers to these questions, because Mörike's web of motivations is too intricate. After all, Nolten's fate is also determined by Agnes' character. Had she herself not been the victim of a neurosis, she might have given Nolten's life a different direction. The novel thus poses more questions than it answers, showing us once more how deeply involved with life's problems its author was at the time of its origin and how much he shunned easy answers.

Mörike had first mentioned the plan of writing an artist novella in 1827. And an early execution was, indeed, his only contribution to the *Damenzeitung* of the brothers Franckh. He continued to work on it after his return to the clergy and was happy to see the work develop into two parts. It was published as a novella with a supplement of musical settings for six of the poems in Stuttgart in August 1832. By 1854 a second edition seemed to be called for. But Mörike would not agree to a simple reprint of the earlier version. He began making corrections and stylistic changes and never finished this work. A younger friend of his, Julius Klaiber, used Mörike's notes for the second part and finished the new edition in 1878. Scholars, however, generally refer to the first edition which preserves the freshness of the moment of creation.[17a]

From the very first line of the novella, "Mozart on the Way to Prague," the reader notices that the author's attitude has changed from the time he wrote *Nolten the Painter.* Now he is overconscientious in giving precise dates and the place of action, showing his interest in the external world as well as the inner experience of his hero. The novella begins as follows: "In the fall of the year 1787, Mozart undertook a journey to Prague in order to have *Don Giovanni* performed there. He was accompanied by his wife.—On the third day of the trip, the fourteenth of September, shortly before eleven o'clock in the morning, the cheerful couple were riding, not much more than thirty hours away from

Vienna, in a northwestern direction beyond the Mangardsberg and the German Thaya near Schrems, where one has almost completely crossed the Moravian Mountains."[18]

The next paragraph offers a detailed description of the yellow-red coach, with flowers and golden ledges on both sides, which the elderly wife of a general, who was proud of her favors to the Mozarts, had lent them. Then Mörike meticulously depicts the costumes of the travelers. And slowly the discussion of external things, and of the forest surrounding them, leads to an analysis of the characters of Mozart and his wife, Constanze. The way this is done could not be more natural and charming. Mörike shows his great artistic skill by letting us partake in a seemingly playful conversation of the couple.

A little incident at the beginning of this conversation has been considered symbolic of the deeper meaning of the entire work. Unawares, Mozart has spilled the perfume of his wife. For a moment she is rather upset. But he consoles her with the remark that they owe the pleasure of the enjoyable last part of the ride to his awkwardness. Before the accident it had been hot, but the perfume had freshened the air. Such light-heartedness is typical for Mozart, who spills his own life and gifts as generously as the perfume; and the reflection of this apparent ease in his music has endeared him to his listeners. This is, however, only one aspect of Mozart's character which Mörike conveys. The light side is inseparably linked to Mozart's melancholic moments, to the threatening loss of his health and the dark sounds in his music. In the novella this is symbolized by the music from *Don Giovanni* which announces the death of the hero.

Long before the significance of the opera becomes clear, however, we read the author's inserted remark: "The painful observation here suggests itself that this impetuous man who was so unbelievably receptive to any allurement of the world and the highest goal within reach of a sensitive mind, forever lacked a constant and pure feeling of self-satisfaction in spite of all he experienced, enjoyed, and created in his short life-span."[19]

A few pages later, the author states:

His health was secretly shaken; an ever returning condition of melancholy was, if not caused, certainly nourished at this point, and thus the premonition of an early death, which finally accompanied him every-where, was unavoidably fulfilled. He was used to grief of all kinds and colors, not excepting the feeling of regret, as a bitter spice of any pleasure. But we know that these sorrows also ran together, clarified and pure, in that deep well which, spouting from a hundred golden tubes, inexhaustible in the variety of its melodies, poured forth all the torment and all the blissfulness of the human heart.[20]

These comments by the author are the abstracts of Mozart's own words to his wife to whom he complains that never before had he found time to enjoy a walk in the forest as he does now during a short stop, and that he had not found the time to play with his children. Now Madame Mozart's character comes into play. Although she has to carry the heaviest burden of their financial problems at home, she cannot bear to see him sink into self-ac-cusations and therefore paints a picture of their future in the gayest colors. On the basis of a slight hope for a position at the Prussian court, she invents so cheerful a vignette of their life there that Mozart's mood changes to one of courage and happiness by the time they arrive at a village where they want to rest and dine.[21]

Mozart leaves Constanze in her room to go for a walk in the park of the nearby castle, the residence of a Count von Schinz-berg. Near a fountain at the entrance he sits down and,

while his ear was comfortably given to the splashing of the water, and his eye fastened on a medium-sized orange-tree, which stood on the ground outside of the row, alone, very close at his side and was loaded with the most beautiful fruits, our friend was soon led upon a lovely reminiscence from his boyhood by this southern view. Smiling con-templatively, he reached for the nearest fruit as if he wanted to feel its wonderful roundness, its juicy coolness in his hollow hand. A musical reminiscence that was almost blotted out was connected with this scene from his youth which emerged again. He followed its uncertain thread for a while, as if he were in a dream. Now his eyes shine, they wander here and there; he is seized by a thought which he pursues eagerly. Absent-mindedly he has reached for the orange once more, it comes off the branch, and remains in his hand. He sees it and sees it not; in-deed, the artist's absent-mindedness goes so far that he—while con-stantly whirling the odorous fruit back and forth under his nose and inaudibly humming now the beginning of a tune, then its middle—at last instinctively pulls an enameled case from the side pocket of his coat, takes out a small knife with a silver handle and slowly cuts through the yellow ball from top to bottom. A faint feeling of thirst might have guided him in this; yet the excited senses were satisfied to inhale the delicious odor. For several minutes he stares at the two inner surfaces, joins them gently, very gently, separates them and joins them again. Then he hears steps nearby, startles, and suddenly becomes aware of where he is and what he has done.[22]

When we compare these sentences with the early rendering of a poetic moment in *Spillner,* we find that the phases of such a moment of creativity are similar. In both instances, an apparently insignificant cause induces a state of mind which Mörike calls insanity or madness in the case of Spillner, and defines as absentmindedness in the Mozart novella. But while he shows us the rapid change of ideas and images in Spillner's mind, he now temporarily withholds the information of what really goes on in Mozart's mind and, instead, directs our eyes to the outer circumstances. We witness the change in Mozart's eyes and his unconscious play with the orange and the knife. Even here we find a minute description of the objects, the silver handle of the knife, and the enameled case, or the roundness and odor of the fruit. This stylistic quality reminds us of the topics of Mörike's later poetry. The interest in objects of nature, daily life, or art, and the close observation of his surroundings has taken the place of earlier self-adulation. And he does not observe only with his eyes but employs the other senses as well: hearing, smell, and even the sense of taste. Indeed, the sound of the water and the growth of the orange tree are doubly reflected—once by Mozart and, again, by the author and the reader.

The moment gains in depth also through the references to the past. This past is, obviously, not a burden and not conducive to melancholy. It puts the composer into the cheerful mood he had hoped for during the previous months. For only such an inner state could enable him to compose the happy duct and chorus of the rural wedding in the first act of *Don Giovanni.* While the past thus influences the creative moment, its essence is still the momentary experience of fulfillment. This is reflected by the constant change of tense in the paragraph. Although the novella is told mainly in the past tense, Mörike cannot help shifting to the present at such an important moment. He seems to catch himself again and returns to the past. But once more he falls into the present when describing Mozart's condition. An intense experience like Mozart's can only be expressed in terms of the present. It comes to an end abruptly and is replaced by a sudden recognition of his offense. Mörike uses a higher degree of "sudden" here with the word *urplötzlich* (all of a sudden), which again shows his predilection for this word.[23]

The novella continues with the indignation of the gardener who discovers what he interprets as a theft. Mozart offers to make amends and sends his card to the owner of the castle and park. He will have to wait a while before he is rescued from his state of being partially a prisoner, since the von Schinzbergs are busy making the last preparations for the betrothal of a beloved niece. Finally the Countess receives the card and at once realizes who is waiting in the garden outside. Mozart is no stranger to the music-loving family and, especially, not to the niece, Eugenie, who has a beautiful voice and likes to sing the maestro's arias. His presence, the Countess feels, would be the most wonderful gift for their celebration. The Count and his son therefore greet him most cordially and invite him to spend the rest of the day and the night at the castle. Mozart, who is easily given to sudden decisions, accepts, and Constanze is fetched from the inn.

What follows is the portrayal of a day amidst the cultured nobility which has the leisure and sensitivity to appreciate Mozart's genius. Mozart himself is surprised by Eugenie's recital of Susanna's aria from *The Marriage of Figaro*. He expresses this most amiably. Then he himself plays one of his concertos which Eugenie has been studying before Mozart's visit.

After the music ends, Mozart entertains the company by relating an episode he witnessed years ago during a visit in Naples. It was this episode he remembered when he was out in the garden picking the orange. The picturesque scene he had observed in Naples was that of games in which more than twenty-four oranges were thrown back and forth between two fishing-boats by beautiful maidens and youths. While the game offered such pleasant diversion for the eyes, his ear was entertained by Sicilian tunes, dances, "Saltarelli, Canzoni a ballo," and so on. Mozart remembered these melodies when he saw the oranges in the Count's garden, and while the melodies went through his mind—intermingled with some of his own—he discovered among them a little dancing tune that he recognized as the piece he needed for his *Don Giovanni*. While he was waiting for the return of the gardener, he wrote it down and now offers it as an engagement present to Eugenie.

At this point, the Count interferes and has the orange tree, which has its own history and special meaning to Eugenie, carried into the room. The tree plays indeed an important role in the novella, being the instigator of Mozart's creative absentmindedness before, and now the cause for a view at the age of the Rococo. Mörike himself calls it "the symbol of this age." Eugenie had long nursed it as a family heirloom from an aunt who had received it from a friend at the French court before its cultured atmosphere was destroyed by the French Revolution. Suddenly the tree had begun to wither and Eugenie had to relinquish all hope for its recovery. Secretly, however, the uncle had put it into the special care of a gardener, who nursed it back to health. For the first time now it was bearing fruits. Their number—nine—had induced the young Count Max to call on the nine Muses and relate the entire story in verses. No wonder, then, that the old Count was, for a moment, upset at seeing the point of these verses blunted by Mozart, who had picked one of the nine oranges. Max, however, quickly changes the ending of his poem and includes Mozart in it as the figure of Apollo, the god of poetry and music and the protector of the Muses.

One blaze of fancy now follows another. In no other work does Mörike give better evidence of the wealth of his imagination. He inserts not only the story of the entertainment in Naples and the history of the orange tree, but also allows Madame Mozart to tell the ladies an episode from their life in Vienna. She relates how Mozart once bought a number of household and garden utensils. One of these, a simple wooden salt-box which can be attached to a wall, Constanze promises Eugenie as a souvenir.

The large number of insertions has been considered, by many critics, as being out of proportion with the main story of Mozart's stay in the house of the von Schinzbergs. The bibliographies give proof of the preoccupation with the problem by listing a number of dissertations and articles on the structure of the novella.[24] But while some earlier critics have found fault with the abundance of anecdotes, which did not seem necessary to the main narrative, the authors of more recent articles come to the defense of the poet. Three approaches to the problem can be recognized in the discussion:

1. Some critics admit the looseness and ease of the construction but justify it as a perfect reflection of Mozart's character, with its playfulness and wealth of ideas. Each one of the anecdotes allows the reader not only a glance at Mozart in various situations but also permits him to see the situations mirrored in Mozart's mind.

2. Others go to the opposite extreme and discover a very strict geometrical organization in the novella to the extent that a similar number of lines can be attributed to certain parts in the first half of the work and to their counterparts in the second half.[25] The structure of the entire work, in this view, would hinge on Mozart's narration of the Naples episode. This central piece would be framed by "the adventure in the castle" (i.e., the picking of the orange and the invitation) and "the celebration of the betrothal" (with the history of the orange tree and the gaiety afterward). A structural parallel is then suggested in the scenes before and after the ones just mentioned: in the conversation between Mozart and Constanze at the beginning, which is interrupted by the author's comments, and, toward the end, in Constanze's tale of the anecdote with the garden tools, which is also interrupted by Mörike's observations. So far so good—but the next layer around these does not support the theory. The scenes following Constanze's tale are much weightier than the very beginning of the novella; they are the climax of the work, and in Mozart's recital of *Don Giovanni* we find the very core of the novella. The critics of the theory of strict geometrical organization have since suggested milder versions, like the division into seven successive parts: exposition, the plucking of the orange, the festivities, Constanze's story, Mozart's recital of *Don Giovanni,* the departure, and the epilogue.[26]

3. Perhaps most fascinating, however, are the attempts to find an analogy in the novella to musical compositions such as the sonata, the symphony, or the opera *Don Giovanni* itself.[27] All these attempts rest on the assumption that the work consists of four parts resembling the four movements in a sonata or sym-

phony. When compared with the opera *Don Giovanni,* which consists of two acts, only two high points can be found in the novella, both centering in the creation of parts of the opera; first the conception of the little song for the rural wedding (during Mozart's state of absentmindedness at the orange tree), second the creation of parts of the finale, with all the horrors of Don Giovanni's meeting with the statue of the dead governor. The contrast between the gay wedding song and the sinister dialogue at the end would thus reflect "the balance of gaiety and tragedy, harmony and conflict pervading Mörike's narrative."[28]

The emphasis on Mörike's affinity for music brought forth yet another valuable contribution to the understanding of the Mozart novella; namely, the idea that the experiences Mörike connected with his hearing of *Don Giovanni* were the germ of the poetic work.[29] Mörike's letters indicate that the deep shock inflicted upon him by the unexpected death of his younger brother August became fused with the deep emotions the opera *Don Giovanni,* which they had heard together a few days before August's death in 1824, had stirred up in him. This was also the year in which he broke off his relationship with Maria Meyer. As time passed, all three experiences were blended. Years later, in 1843, the poet called them his *noli me tangere* past, the past he had tried to suppress. The fact that he could mention it at this point, after he had heard some of the lighter pieces of *Don Giovanni* sung by the wife of his friend David Strauß, is the first indication of a process in the course of which the suppressed memories became the inspiration for the Mozart novella. Mörike's own sorrowful past feeds the representation of Don Giovanni's anguish in the face of horror and death.

To return to the novella: the hosts had reminded Mozart of his promise to acquaint them with his newest work, *Don Giovanni.* And so he begins by playing several parts of it on the piano, occasionally singing the arias himself. Eugenie's attentive listening and her fiancé's penetrating remarks about the music excite him, and finally he offers to play the part of the finale that no one has heard yet. As a transition to his performance he describes the moments of conception of the music that was to express Don Giovanni's encounter with the statue of the governor. The immediate inspiration had come from the revised libretto for these scenes which he had found unexpectedly on his desk one night. Although he usually did not work ahead but tried to compose one part after another, he felt he had to make an exception here. He composed the chorale for the governor which Mörike describes in the following words: "The sounds seem to fall down through the blue night from silver trumpets, icy-cold, cutting to the quick and soul, as if they were coming from distant stellar worlds."[30]

After this Mozart continues by telling his audience that the later scene between Don Giovanni and the statue which leads to the hero's death was created at the same time. And as he begins to play this also, the reader of the novella again finds the music transformed into images which can be rendered in words. More than that, he hears about the effect which this music has on its audience, as in the following sentences:

And when now Don Giovanni, defying the eternal power with an enormous wilfulness, struggles helplessly under the growing pressure of the infernal powers, resists and squirms and finally perishes, still with the full expression of greatness in every gesture—whose heart would not tremble with delight and fear at one and the same time? It is a sensation similar to that with which one admires the grand spectacle of an unruly natural power, the burning of a splendid ship. Reluctantly we side with its blind greatness, so to speak, and, crunching, share its pain in the violent course of its self-destruction.[31]

To the extent that words can express the meaning of Mozart's music, Mörike here approaches perfection. The image of the sounds falling from silver trumpets, icy-cold, through the blue night, reminds us of the poem "An Wilhelm Hartlaub."[32] And Don Giovanni's struggle could not be painted more vividly than by the quick succession of verbs like defy, struggle, resist, and squirm, together with the expressions of growing pressure. The greatness of the struggle is underlined by the strength of the opposing forces, the eternal order and the infernal powers. (The image of fire recurs throughout the novella: for example in the form of Mount Vesuvius as a background for the Naples episode, and in Eugenie's mind as an inner flame that consumes Mozart.[33]) A man who could create such contrasts must have had tremendous strength or must have expended all the energy he had. The latter was true of Mozart, in Mörike's view. Asked by the Countess how he felt after he had finished working on this part of the opera, he admits: "I said to myself: if you died this night and had to leave your score at this point, would it give you peace in the grave?"[34]

With this sentence, we are again reminded of the motif that runs through the novella: the presentiment of Mozart's early death. This is so closely woven into the whole narration that the reader gains the impression of an inevitable union of genius and death. If we glance back at Mörike's other works with the artist as hero, we find the same fusion in *Nolten the Painter* and in "Erinna to Sappho." But while Nolten experiences death as a fateful power beyond all human understanding, Mozart and Erinna carry its image with them and try to acquaint themselves with it. They both love life and still wish to create works of art. They do not long for death as Nolten and Larkens before their end, when they do not see how they could continue to live. No, for Mozart and Erinna death would mean an unwished-for and abrupt end. But they have to live with this threat and are aware of it without being consoled. Mozart, it is true, finds some comfort in the thought that no impostor would be able to pass the unfinished opera off as his own composition, because Mozart's friends would recognize his stamp.

The novella as a whole, however, ends on a note of impending tragedy.[35] Eugenie fears that Mozart "would burn himself out, quickly and unavoidably, in his own flames, that he could only be a passing figure on earth, because it actually could not bear the profusion he would abound in."[36]

The others try to dispel any "notion of misfortune," but when Eugenie returns to the room with the piano, she accidentally finds a sheet of paper with a little Bohemian folk song that becomes an oracle which she applies to Mozart:

> A little fir-tree greens, somewhere,
> Who knows, deep in the forest,
> A rose-bush, who can tell
> Within what garden.
> They are already picked,
> O soul, remember,
> Upon your grave to root
> And to grow tall.

Two sable colts are grazing
In the meadow,
They come back home to town
Lustily prancing.
They will go step by step
With your dead body;
Perhaps, perhaps before
The shoes are loosened
From hoofs, where now I
See them shining brightly![37]

More consistently than *Nolten the Painter,* the Mozart novella concentrates on depicting the character of an artist, his creative moments, and the danger for the artist himself inherent in the close relationship with the demonic sources of creativeness. We do not witness the early death of Mozart, however, but rather a climactic moment in his career, just before one of his greatest triumphs, the first performance of *Don Giovanni* in Prague. The tragic threat of demonic powers, which carry Don Giovanni to his doom, is held in suspense in the case of Mozart. His melancholy is balanced by happy moods and sparkling, joyful moments. This joyfulness is supported in the novella by the cheerful surroundings at the Schinzberg castle. All the objects that appear in the novella bear out the spirit of the Rococo age: delicate artfulness that intends to make life more beautiful and enjoyable. Before the French Revolution only a few people knew that these endeavors would soon prove to be in vain. Against this background, the Mozart of the novella appears symbolic of his whole age—both are in the zenith of existence, expressing their wealth in an abundance of artistic forms, and both are threatened by an impending end.

If Mörike succeeded so well in reflecting the spirit of that age, his success is due to his change of attitude toward the outside world since the time of writing his earlier artist novel. In *Nolten* he had not paid much attention to artifacts and objects of daily life. But his poetry had shown a growing concern with the things that surrounded him. With this new attentiveness he now depicted Mozart's coach and his garden tools, the garden at the Rococo castle and its furnishings and the inhabitants' costumes. The earlier novel had shown traits of Romanticism and elements that seemed to foreshadow the twentieth century. The Mozart novella, on the other hand, reflects the attitude of the *Biedermeier* era that cherished the Classical and Romantic heritage and developed a sensitivity for artistic values similar to that of the Rococo.[38]

II *"Lucie Gelmeroth" and the Fragments of Two Novels*

Nolten the Painter was Mörike's earliest prose work and also the one that occupied his mind the longest. If we leave the revision of the novel out of this account, however, then "Mozart on the Way to Prague" was his last work in prose. Between the years 1832 and 1856 he wrote another novella, "Lucie Gelmeroth" (published in 1834), and began two novels, one (untitled) with English personages (during the years 1833–36), perhaps in connection with the first version of "Lucie Gelmeroth," whose original name was Miss Jenny Harrower, and the second, the "Geschichte von der Silbernen Kugel, oder der Kupferschmied von Rothenburg," (Story of the Silver Ball,) at some time between 1843 and 1851.

The finished novella "Lucie Gelmeroth" indicates a more courageous tackling of life's difficulties than was noticeable in *Nolten the Painter*. It is also a psychological study. But while all the figures in *Nolten the Painter* succumb to the intricacies of their character and fate, Lucie Gelmeroth—with the loving help of the narrator—overcomes her affliction and finds her way back into life.

The story forms part of the unpublished memoirs of the narrator, a German scholar. During a visit to his home town, after a long absence, he hears that Lucie Gelmeroth, with whom he has played as a child, has confessed to having killed her deceased sister's former fiancé. Everyone in town knows that the faithlessness of the second lieutenant had, indeed, caused the sister's death. (Anna, one could say, was similar in some respects to Agnes, Elisabeth, and Constanze in the earlier novel.) But nobody believes Lucie capable of such revenge. She, however, insists that she has caused the death of the second lieutenant, whose body had been found in a lonely garden not far from the town; and she demands her own death as a punishment. She so strongly insists on her own death that the investigators cannot help suspecting that her longing for death was the real reason for her confession. Hoping that she would change her mind and that the real killer would be found, they put Lucie in jail and are only too happy to let the narrator visit her and try to influence her. To explain his concern with Lucie's condition, the narrator then inserts two little episodes from their childhood, which show his early sympathy for the girl.

The episodes can also be understood as being symbolic of their present situation. The first one shows the two children on a pony that gets out of hand when a little theatrical performance is interrupted by a thunderstorm. They are straying in a labyrinth, just as the grown-up Lucie has lost her way in the thicket of life. In the second episode, Lucie is erroneously accused of a theft. The accusation makes her mysteriously attractive to the narrator, so that his feelings are mixed when her innocence is discovered. The similarity with the present situation is even more obvious.

As soon as the narrator is alone with Lucie in her cell, she asks him for his advice and tells him what has happened to her after her sister's death. An earlier friend of the sister had come to her, and they mourned their loss together. Upon parting, Lucie had uttered the words, "Avenge the sister if you are a man!" without thinking of anything definite. A few days later she had heard of the second lieutenant's death and received word from the friend that he had killed him in an honest duel. This had only increased her despair, since she had blamed herself for the deed and for the danger it meant to the fugitive. She was longing for death herself but had shied away from suicide—in this predicament it occurred to her that she could seek death from the hands of justice. In the meantime, however, she had begun to realize how untenable her position was. She was ready to tell the truth but was afraid of living with the disgrace it would bring on her.

Since Mörike is mainly interested in the girl's mental state, he does not lose much time having the case solved and her released, after which he describes her inner condition: "But now her inner state demanded the most loving, delicate care. She believes herself dishonored, annihilated in the eyes of the world, ridiculed as an adventuress, pitied as a paranoiac. Involuntarily she returns to human life insensible and resigned. The future lies before her like an infinite desert, and she sees herself as an empty despicable lie; she does not know what to do with herself."[39]

At this moment, she has gone beyond the paranoia of Agnes and Elisabeth, who derived some comfort from an *idée fixe*. Like Larkens and Nolten she has reached the point of utter forlornness. But unlike them, she receives outside help of a deeper value than friends and acquaintances can offer. Nolten had lost his love, whereas Lucie's will grow out of this experience. The narrator takes her to the home of a relative, a country parson, where Lucie slowly recovers; and two years later she becomes the narrator's wife.

Mörike called the work a novella, and justifiably so. In its brevity it comes much closer than "Mozart" to the model of the stories in Boccaccio's *Decameron*.

The novel, of which we have nine fragments of various lengths, was to be set partly in England, partly in Germany. As in "Lucie Gelmeroth" the narrator introduces himself as a German scholar. He meets the heroes of the novel on the estate of his uncle, Killford, a retired university professor. Killford's main interest is the natural sciences. With this scientific interest, Mörike adds a new dimension to this novel, which seems to have been planned on a wider scope than his other works. How genuine was the author's own involvement in the scientific occupations of some of his figures is much harder to judge than in the case of his Austrian contemporary Adalbert Stifter, with whom he shares the designation of a *Biedermeier* poet. Stifter was definitely aware of science and in some works indicated an appreciation of its development that would disrupt the quiet world of the *Biedermeier*. In any event, it shows a certain open-mindedness on Mörike's part to let Killford be as well-versed in the sciences as he is in ancient literature.

The professor is not the central figure, however. He is only the host of some more important personages: Mary, the daughter of the English Baronet Leithem, and Master Thomas, the former tutor of the Baronet's son. Master Thomas shares Killford's interest in the sciences but arouses Killford's antipathy by reading a large number of religious tracts. He writes about religious questions, and is preparing himself to become a missionary. He is engaged to the maid of the Baronet's second wife, and his main task in the fragments of the novel is to acquaint the narrator with the previous life of the Leithem family. The most striking aspect of his reports is the predominance of religious problems and struggles.

One of the fragments, for example, concentrates on the young Viennese Countess Helene, the Baronet's bride. She is about to convert from Catholicism to Protestantism and receives religious instruction from a young man who plans to become a minister. This young man's confessions are inserted in the fragment. While discussing religion with the young Countess, he falls in love with her. But at the same time he begins to doubt the dogmas which he is explaining to her, and is thrown into despair. Suddenly he sees himself as a thief trying to rob the young Countess of her most valuable possession, the fragrance and brightness of her religion, Catholicism, which must be especially dear to her, since her beloved mother had died as a devout Catholic.

A similar emotional conflict occurs in Mary, the Baronet's daughter. The predominant feature of her character is her imagination. In connection with it, her religious emotions first develop in a manner quite agreeable to her Protestant father. But then a relative of her mother comes for a visit and softly intimates her concern over the wrong upbringing of the girl. This causes an inner struggle in Mary, which makes itself felt to the others in violent emotional outbursts which are interpreted as part of her fantastic nature. In reality, she is torn between her old, tender feelings for her father and a new antipathy for him, because she begins to think that he should have sacrificed his faith to his love for her mother.

Mary's difficulties find an additional explanation in two other fragments. One of them begins with the description of a rather exotic scene. In a cave hidden by bushes, stones, and moss, the Baronet and his company find a handsome boy, about thirteen years old, half-naked and sleeping next to a cage with exotic birds and a beautiful snake. They awaken him and hear that he is deeply worried whether he has injured one of the village boys who had hidden his clothes and tried to steal his parrot. The Baronet consoles him, has him brought to his house and dressed in fine clothes, and presents him to his companions. They all welcome the beautiful, well-behaved stranger; only Mary shies away from him. Once again, the others explain that as one of her fancies. They do not know that she herself discovered the boy in the cave when she was out in the woods alone and hoped to keep this encounter to herself. To her it was a vision and a beautiful dream, and she did not want this to become part of the real everyday world.

The Baronet's efforts on behalf of the boy, Alexis, prove to be well-spent. He turns out to be the illegitimate son of an English nobleman, who had run away from a Swiss school because of the harsh treatment, and who eagerly seized his father's offer to attend a military academy. At the time of the narrator's visit to Professor Killford's estate, this education has come to an end and Alexis/Victor is seen at the scene of a fire near the estate, where he shows courage and self-assurance. His presence has been kept secret from Mary in order not to give nourishment to her fantastic attachment to the young man. Yet it is generally understood that Mary and Victor will marry some day.

In another fragment, Mary's love for Victor is shown in a truly fantastic setting. Like an oriental princess, she is lying on a rug with a pattern that reminds her of the cave where she first saw Victor. Her favorite servants, an old Scotchman and his wife keep her company. The two have been Mary's companions from her childhood, and the old man's stories and fairy tales have had a strong influence on the development of her mind. In the eyes of a sober man like Master Thomas, they have exerted an unfortunate influence, since she showed anyhow "a [pathological] (brackets in the manuscript) inclination, to raise the imagination to the position of being the only organ of all [inner life]. It is as if she sees the world through colored glass, therefore her passionate bent [lacuna], invention of fairy tales, etc."[40]

No doubt, Mörike could draw on his own inclinations for many aspects of Mary's character. A certain leaning toward the more colorful practices in the Catholic Church, which give better nourishment to the imagination of the poet than the Protestant services, had also been alloted to Nolten. This leaning toward Catholicism also makes itself felt in Mörike's letters and may have played a role in his later love for Gretchen Speeth. And what is Mary's "colored glass" other than Mörike's own gift to poeticize and to invent fairy tales! Master Thomas continues his criticism of such inclinations by speaking of "romantic abundance and that antipathy against the [naked] truth" and thereby provides an argument for some of Mörike's critics who write of his fear of reality and his hiding behind the masks of his fairy tales. But Mörike must not be identified with his creations, and we also cannot tell from the fragments whether or not Mörike was going to reconcile his heroine with reality.

"The Story of the Silver Ball" or "The Coppersmith of Rothenburg" must have been projected by Mörike between 1843 and 1851. The very sketchy outline indicates that the plot and the characters would have been very different from the works we have discussed so far. It is true that Mörike read a voluminous biography of Mozart before he wrote the novella. But in his own work he did not exhibit his knowledge in a scholarly way but created an episode whose truth rests on the value of his poetic vision. In the outline for "The Story of the Silver Ball," the author's bookish knowledge about the city of Rothenburg remains distinct from the characters, who do not seem to belong to any particular age. This may, of course, be the fault of the original draft. But while a glance into Mörike's workshop at the time of the conception of the novel concerning the Baronet Leithem's family has shown us the author's original concern with the psychology of his figures still taking shape, the story of Rothenburg presents itself as a tableau with two fixed elderly characters who do not promise to change. The woman is most interested in enlarging her fortune, and her husband's dominant character trait is orderliness.

As a good representative of the *Biedermeier* period, Mr. Knisel, the husband, loves to collect minerals, plants, coleopters, and all things referring to the history and topography of Rothenburg. And Mörike himself must have studied the latter rather carefully, for two of the six short sketches consist of detailed descriptions of the city and references to historical events. The reader may well see in this interest for the city the nucleus of the novel. In the same way, his fairy tale of "The Stuttgart Hutzelmännlein" may have grown out of his love for the citizens of Stuttgart. But obviously the simple plot of a young shoemaker who leaves his home town, finds a false love in another town and returns to Stuttgart to find the right bride, proved a more ade-

quate vehicle for Mörike's imagination than the plot of the unfinished "Story of the Silver Ball." There was to be a chest with a
valuable silver dinner set that had been entrusted to Mrs. Knisel.
She was to find it difficult to part with it at the assigned moment
in favor of the true heir, a young girl. The confusion of the years
of the Napoleonic Wars were to have an influence and would
have given a chance for the painting of a broader picture. But
Mörike did not continue to work on it. We know that the reason
for leaving this work unfinished was not a total lack of productivity, for he did publish "The Stuttgart Hutzelmännlein" in
1852, "The Hand of Jezerte" in 1853, and "Mozart on the Way
to Prague" in 1856 as a result of his efforts during the preceding
years.

III *Mörike's Fairy Tales*

In 1836 Mörike published "Der Schatz" (The Treasure),
which he designated as a "novella." Three years later, however,
in the foreword to the second edition, he used the term "fairy
tale." The ambiguity of the title is related to the story, which
also is ambiguous. Again and again, one feels the author's effort
to explain his hero's dreams and experiences on the trip to Frankfurt (where he is to buy the jewels for a precious crown he is assigned to make) psychologically. But on the other hand, the
principal characters are so strongly guided by their faith in the
existence of certain legendary figures that the supernatural seems
to project into real life. Legendary or fairy tale figures, like
ghosts, dwarfs, and speaking animals appear to the characters in
the story when they are either under the influence of alcohol, are
ill (scarlet fever), or when they are asleep. Everything that happens to the hero in "The Treasure" could be naturally explained
and the story would then be correctly termed a novella, i.e., a narration of unheard-of events. But the characters themselves believe in the supernatural and make it a force that must be reck-
oned with and which influences the course of events. Thus the
faith in the one hundred rules—and a few additional ones for
special occasions—which the hero, on the day of his confirmation,
finds in the little book called "Jewel-box," runs through the story
like a red thread. The good luck of the hero, who wins his bride
and an envied position in society without any effort simply be-

cause he was born on an Easter Sunday, transposes us into a fairy tale world.

The hero, Arbogast, tells most of the story to entertain a circle of ladies and gentlemen assembled in the dining room of the best hotel in the spa K. He is now fifty years old, a *Hofrat* at the court and still the object of curiosity to the other guests, who cannot understand how the boy of modest background, a goldsmith's journeyman, had been able to reach this present position. *Hofrat* Arbogast finally agrees to tell his story.

As a young man, he had won the confidence of his older cousin, in whose shop he was working. The cousin, because of his trust in the youth, sent him to Frankfurt with four hundred gold coins to buy the precious stones they needed for the crown of the Princess von Astern, who was to become the king's bride. On the second day of his trip, Arbogast discovered that the money had been stolen from his knapsack. Before he could arouse the innkeeper and the police, his little book of sayings, the "Jewel-box," got into his hands, he leafed through it and found the rule:

> Whatever is stolen from you on St. Gorgon's day,
> You can fetch again before St. Cyprian's day;
> Do not hunt for it, don't make any noise,
> And, be sure to be careful.

Since the theft had occurred on St. Gorgon's day, he decided to follow this advice and keep still. But a few days later his confidence began to wane; he became nervous for fear his cousin would send the police after him, and left the inn in order to walk across the border, where he might hide with distant relatives. Arbogast continues his story with the account of a sudden change in his fortunes: "But the miraculous fate, under whose guidance I stood, now announced itself in a very strange manner."[41]

While crossing a barren heath, he saw a shepherd in the distance and shouted to him asking for the way. Before he could receive an answer, however, he heard the signpost behind him clap its wooden hands; and when he looked around, he discovered that the post had changed its position so that one arm pointed into the valley, the other was hanging straight down. Frightened by this ghostly vision, Franz Arbogast ran to the shepherd who pointed to a different direction than that indicated by the signpost and warned him against walking down into the valley to the haunted castle. But fog fell and Franz Arbogast found himself circling on the heath and finally walking downward. In the end he is glad to reach the castle in the valley that may offer some shelter after all. Could he explain his straying with the few drinks from the bottle in his knapsack? Or was he under a magic spell?

There was no sense in running any further that night. He knocked at the door of the house steward, gave a false name and profession—for he was still in fear of persecution because of the four hundred gold pieces that had disappeared—and received lodging grudgingly. The next day was a Sunday, and the steward and his wife left him in the care of their niece while they went to church. Oddly enough, the niece Josephe did not seem to believe the name he had given nor his fabricated stories of some flirtations in town. After several hours she confessed knowing him intimately but would not reveal her own identity. He intensely wished to remember why she looked familiar to him, but his memory forsook him. The presence of this girl made him understand for the first time what attraction a young girl might have for a young man.

That night he had a strange dream of fairy tale character that fitted right into his daytime experiences. He saw a gigantic map of Europe and, marching along on it, a goblin who was happy to pause for a little conversation with him. In the course of their talk, the goblin intimated that he was trying to find a person born on an Easter Sunday who was destined to help redeem the ghost of the haunted castle, the evil Countess Irmel, ancestress of the Princess of Astern, for whom Franz Arbogast was to make a new crown. To Franz, the goblin's talk revealed valuable information in connection with his stay at the castle, since he himself was such an Easter child. As the dream continued, he received further hints that were to help him solve his daytime problems. Upon the goblin's invitation, he watched from afar a festivity that another tribe of goblins was holding in a nearby village. The tribe, so his confidant told him, held possession of Irmel's treasure and skilfully added to it whatever gold came in its reach. Of course, Franz was to look in this valley for his four hundred gold pieces as soon as he would get a chance.

No wonder that he awoke quite happily the next morning, hoping that he would bring his adventures to a fortunate end. His strain of luck continued when he accidentally touched a little thimble he had long carried around with him, reminding him of a childhood love who had given it to him. Finally it dawned on him why Josephe had looked so familiar; she was Ännchen, little Anne, with whom he had played as a boy. She had lived in the same house with him but had died of scarlet fever, mainly because her foster parents had not taken very good care of her. At least, this was what the adults believed. Franz, however, should have known better, since Mrs. Lichtlein, the woman who was to lay out the dead, had half assured him that his friend would recover. He had secretly sneaked into Anne's sickroom and met not only Mrs. Lichtlein but also the frightening fairy Scarlatina, a woman with red skirt and shoes, a black cap, and an extremely pale face which blushed once in a while. His mother explained this vision, when he told it to her, as the first indication that he would also come down with the sickness and ordered him to stay in his room. From the window, he saw Mrs. Lichtlein and a helper take a long, heavy bundle out of Anne's room at night and was convinced that they were going to bring his friend back to health. He had never been able to make sure of this, though, because she had not returned to the house. Only now could he guess that she had been taken from his home town and lived in the steward's house, at least for some time. He could hardly await the moment when he could tell Anne of his discovery.

Yet his joy was blurred as soon as he left his room and went to the steward's quarters. There a number of people from the neighboring village were waiting for him as the one who was wanted for the theft of the four hundred gold pieces. He was thrown into the tower to await the arrival of the owner of the estate. The Baron, however, appeared as the all-knowing benefactor. He was the brother of the noble lady who had presented Franz with his book of rules, knowing that he was an Easter child and might be of help to Irmel, who ought to come to rest finally. She had also taken Anne's destiny into her hand. Now that the noble lady was dead, the Baron continued her efforts.

He released Franz and promised him Anne's hand as soon as the ghost was paid.

Here the *Hofrat* breaks off his narration, leaving the completion of the story to the imagination of his guests. One of them, an imaginative young lady, suggests that the lovers must have discovered Irmel's treasure on the next day. With it must have been the torn necklace, upon the repair of which the ghost's rest depended. Franz put it together again and dropped it into the river, whereupon Irmel found her peace. Then Mörike lets another listener tell of a famous robber who could have gathered the treasure to which some thief might have added Franz Arbogast's gold pieces, thus offering a more realistic turn of the story. In order to show that he is playing with his readers, Mörike follows this up with another turn to the fairy-tale-like explanation that the signpost was none other than the bewitched adulterous lover of Irmel, also waiting for release. This interplay of supernatural and realistic explanations lifts the entire story to a level of sophistication that would be foreign to a folk fairy tale. And more so than in such a tale we become acquainted with the thoughts of the story's figures. But they are generally very näive in accepting whatever fortune befalls them and are not as complex as the heroes of many Romantic fairy tales. In this they do resemble the simple people in the folk stories—they are also related, however, to the persons in Mörike's best known tale, "The Stuttgart Hutzelmännlein."

In 1839, three years after "The Treasure," Mörike published another fairy tale, "Der Bauer und sein Sohn" (The Farmer and His Son), which represents a very different type of writing. It resembles the moralistic almanac stories which constituted the chief reading material of the less educated classes at the time. It may well be that personal observations of cruelties had tempted Mörike into writing this story against the maltreatment of animals.

The farmer Peter used to beat his horse and feed it poorly. One morning he wakes up covered with blue spots which his wife interprets as a punishment. The warning goes unheeded, though, and Peter finally discovers that the horse has disappeared from the stable. On an invisible meadow the horse is allowed to recover, whereupon the king finds it and presents it to his wife because it is so handsome. In the meantime, Peter has met with one misfortune after another; he has taken to drinking and lost his home. Frieder, his son, is tending the goats when the king's retinue visits the village in the course of a hunt. He arouses attention by claiming that the queen's horse is his father's and is asked to prove it by riding the horse in a circle around the meadow, which would become his own if he succeeded. Thus far the horse had refused to carry anybody but the queen, but it well remembers Frieder's secret kind deeds of years ago and helps him win the land and the king's favor. This turn of events finally brings the father Peter to his senses, and from then on they live as a happy family.

"The Stuttgart Hutzelmännlein" was published in 1852, during the early happy stage of Mörike's married life in Stuttgart. More than any other work, this fairy tale breathes his love for the simple people, for his native country, and for fairy-tale motifs. It is related to the "Idyl from Lake Constance," which mirrors the life of shepherds and fishermen. But in the "Idyl" the heroic meter (the hexameter) gave the simplicity a touch of the exemplary or classical, while the prose of the "Hutzelmännlein" is so mixed with words and rhymes from the Swabian dialect that it comes realistically close to the popular language. Mörike felt obliged to help his readers with twelve pages of explanations of Swabian expressions and folklore elements in an appendix which lists such words as *Hutzelbrot* (bread made of dried pears, figs, and nuts) or *Lichtbraten* (roast to which the masters of a craft invited their journeymen at the beginning of the winter), etc. In some instances, he mentions the source of his information, such as "the historiographer of the Emperor Maximilian," so that the reader receives the impression that he is presented with a scholarly work.

The impression that the tale is based on realistic elements is deepened by the description of geological formations in the region of the hero's journey. Most interesting in this respect is the so-called *Blautopf*, halfway between the tributaries of the Rhine on the one side and those of the Danube on the other. The mountain range in this region—the Swabian Albs—consists of limestone. So soft is this stone that the waters have eroded it subterraneously, bringing about many stalactitic formations. In certain places, glacial deposits force these subterranean waters to the surface, as is the case in the *Blautopf*, a bowl containing about 7,194 cubic yards and being approximately twenty-four yards in depth. It feeds a lively little tributary of the Danube, the Blau. The water is of a clear blue color, especially after a period of good weather. No wonder that it gave rise to many popular beliefs, such as the one that it is without bottom or very hot deeper down.

It is against this background that Mörike invented his story of the beautiful nymph Lau, which he inserted in the "Hutzelmännlein." Lau is the wife of an old water-sprite who resides in the Danube close to the Black Sea. He has exiled her because she bore him only dead children; and her mother-in-law had prophesied that she would not have a healthy child until she had laughed five times (she was always sad without reason). Now she lives in the *Blautopf* with her maids and is known to the people as the beautiful and evil Lau, because she makes the waters spill over into the village when she is in bad humor.

Such motivation of her actions is characteristic of this fairy tale. Mörike does not stress the supernatural power of the elemental spirit but rather lets her act like a temperamental human being. Thus she is not in search of a human soul but hopes for healthy children.[42]

The beautiful Lau is cured with the help of the family in the nearby inn. She is able to visit them by climbing out of the well in their basement and taking part in some of their daily activities. And here the story abounds in charming details of the life of the villagers, as if the author had almost forgotten his goal and had been carried away by his imagination. One spell of laughter, for example, is caused by tiny Hans who is sitting on the "potty" on top of the huge bed of his parents, another during a gathering in the spinning room by the confusion that results when they all tried to say the tongue-twister: " 's leit a Klötzle Blei glei bei Blaubeuren." In the end, the nymph returns to the Black Sea with great splendor, leaving her friends a few valuable gifts. She promises to renew the gifts so that they could hand out three presents every hundred years to the first three traveling journeymen coming to the inn.

These presents form the connecting link between the Lau's story and the tale of the Stuttgart *Hutzelmännlein* and his protégé Seppe, the wandering shoemaker. Seppe is one of the three to receive such a gift, a beautiful cap for his future bride. More important than this, however, is the plummet, the "*Klötzlein Blei*" of the tongue-twister mentioned above. This plummet contains the tooth of some fabulous fish, which had the power to make the person who carried it on his left side invisible. It had once been in the possession of the Lau but was stolen from her, and was supposed to be lying somewhere in the vicinity of the *Blautopf*. The hero, Seppe, is commissioned to find this plummet for the *Hutzelmännlein* when they part during the night before Seppe leaves Stuttgart.

This is a fairy tale motif so natural and so closely related to popular tales that Mörike's friends were convinced the author had made use of an already existing folk legend. But Mörike denied having any knowledge of similar traditions.[43] We must, therefore, attribute the wealth of his inventions in the "Hutzelmännlein" once more to his gift of inventing myths of a kind that are otherwise known as property of the people. That is true also of the following details of his story: upon their farewell, the *Hutzelmännlein,* who reaches only to the waist of the hero, hands Seppe a *Hutzelbrot* that will always grow again, as long as he does not eat the last bit. Other objects with magic power are the two pairs of shoes he is given, one for himself and one for leaving somewhere to be found by the girl who will some day bring happiness to him. The shoes were made by the *Hutzelmännlein,* the patron of the craft of the shoemakers, and are supposed to bring good luck to whoever wears them.

But in Seppe's case the shoes do not prove very beneficial until the end of the story, because by mistake he puts on one of the girl's shoes, leaving one of his to her. One of his feet is therefore constantly trying to make the motion of stepping on the pedal of a spinning wheel, which he misinterprets as an urge to become a shear-grinder or turner. And while the lucky shoe brings him to the inn at the *Blautopf* in time to receive a present, the unlucky one may be blamed for making him miss the plummet until his return trip and possibly even for the misfortune he encounters in the city of Ulm.

As in many other fairy tales, the hero's wanderings do not lead directly to his goal, the beautiful bride, wealth, or power. The protective guidance of the wise patron cannot prevent his coming in touch with Evil and endangering his life. In Mörike's tale, Evil and Death are personified by a woman, the good-looking widow of an Ulm shoemaker, in whose workshop Seppe finds employment. His magic shoes, to be sure, make an awful noise at night, trying to warn him, but he puts a big rock on them because he has already fallen in love. Two months later, he cannot hide his feelings any longer and—in a situation typical of Mörike's humor—while he is hanging some hams in the chimney, he admits that he would like to become her husband. She does not reject him, and thus he descends from the ladder with a big sooty spot on his nose and kisses her for the first time. In the evening, he presents her with the beautiful cap, the Lau's gift, and lets her try his *Hutzelbrot*. Upon her questioning, he tells her of his patron and about some of his pranks, not noticing that she is bored with the naïveté of these tales. Indeed, so blind is he in his confidence and love for her that he allows her to feed the last bite of the bread to her parrot. This delicacy brings out an unsuspected gift of the bird: he talks. But again Seppe does not heed his warning—"Who killed one and two, will also kill the third." Only the woman turns white as the wall and cannot regain her composure for the rest of the evening.

The next morning, the bird is dead. The woman's offhand attitude puzzles Seppe. But it still takes the straightforward accusation of one of his companions before he recognizes the danger he is in. His fiancée is said to have poisoned her two former husbands. Seppe is dumbfounded. Tottering, he follows his companions; in his mind, though, he thanks God, who has saved him in time, and decides to leave Ulm that night. The question is where to go. He is without money and has lost his magic bread. Should he return to Stuttgart in so poor a condition? Would not his friends there laugh about him? But this still seems better than to go anywhere else, for all places but home now appear sad and miserable to him. Thus he dons the *Hutzelmännlein* shoes and begins his return trip. At this point, Mörike inserts a few remarks of charming humor in the popular vein which show his superior attitude in respect to his modest, inexperienced hero: "He ... took his hurting heart, pressed it with soft hands back into shape, as the housewives do with a little chicken that has been stepped on, and in the end his consolation and last conclusion amounted to a saying of his cousin's: 'There have been only three good women: one drowned in the bath, one ran out of the world, they are still looking for the third.' "[44]

His left shoe is bothering him again. He therefore exchanges it for a boot from his knapsack and, henceforth, does not meet with any further adversities. Not far from the *Blautopf*, his right shoe refuses to go any further; he looks around and finds the plummet. That improves his mood considerably. He forgets his heart-breaking experience in Ulm, as he tries the fabulous tooth's power on his further journey, first on a farmer who refuses to let him ride on his wagon and now has to drive him anyhow; then on a young man, a dyer, who had made a fool of him when he came this way several months ago. He finds the young man standing next to some fabrics he has dyed and layed out on the meadow to dry, approaches him unseen, grasps him and wraps him in his fabrics like a baby in its bundle. And to the great surprise of the villagers, the dyer then floats through the air, crying for help, and finally lands on the square before the church.

Coming closer to his home town, Seppe learns to his delight that his early return to Stuttgart might easily be overlooked because of the festivities on the occasion of Count Eberhard's silver wedding and his daughter's marriage. And indeed, he is able to slip through the crowds and find food and loving care—above all a bed for rest—in the house of an older cousin. The motherly woman promises to provide him with a costume for tomorrow's mummery and tells him that the neighbor's girl, Vrone Kiderlen, has just borrowed some clothes for the same purpose.

And here it is time for us to find out what has happened to the other pair of shoes which Seppe had placed on the banister of a bridge in Stuttgart before he left. Mörike himself picks up this second strain of his story much earlier, namely at the time when Seppe meets the false bride in Ulm and is falling in love with her. As if to balance Seppe's involvement with the evil power, from which he was to extricate himself at the last minute, Mörike tells his readers of the pretty, judicious girl, Vrone Kiderlen, who has found the shoes and accepts them as a birthday gift from some well-meaning power.

But Vrone's experiences with the shoes are not very fortunate either. Because of the wrong shoe, she jumps so awkwardly on the dance floor and falls so often that her companions shake their heads. Her mother is the first to blame the shoes for these troubles and sends her to a shoemaker to try on some other ones. The man recognizes the nature of her shoes at once and cannot resist the temptation of having his own daughter steal them from Vrone. But the *Hutzelmännlein's* revenge for this theft befalls him on the following night; all the shoes he is storing in the attic are thrown into the lake. He quickly returns the magic shoes to Vrone's house, where the *Hutzelmännlein* retains them for a later moment in the story. Until then Vrone can be her old happy self.

With Seppe's return, the time has come for the *Hutzelmännlein* to carry his schemes to a happy ending. Overnight he outfits Seppe with a much fancier costume than the cousin could have done, and has the magic tooth taken out of the plummet and mounted in gold. As we see later, he has been similarly active on Vrone's behalf. And so the two young people, who had known each other as neighbors before Seppe's journey, are now ready to meet under the most extraordinary circumstances and discover the very simple truth that the beloved whom Seppe had thought to find in the distance had been so close to him all his life.

For these extraordinary circumstances, Mörike once more lets his imagination roam. Describing details of the mummery, he prepares the reader for Seppe's part in it. Half unconsciously, the young man has moved closer and closer to the rope on which a group of entertainers are showing their skills before the Count and his guests. When the dancers are done, a peculiar little man, who is wearing a mask, surprises everyone by showing much greater skills on the rope. His goal is to attract attention for his announcement that anybody could win what was in the sack he has hung up high by following his example. Who else could he be but the *Hutzelmännlein* who was preparing the way for his protégés, to whom he wanted to call the Count's attention. Seppe's feet have been itching all this time to get on the rope. When he steps on it, though, he discovers to his surprise a second person at the other end, dressed in a similar costume but hiding behind a mask.

At first, they are both slow and uncertain. But after the second person accidentally removes the mask and Seppe sees the lovely Vrone opposite himself, he takes the *Hutzelmännlein's* advice, invites her to exchange the ill-fitting shoes, and now they move on with such ease that the crowds cheer and the Count expresses the wish to meet them. This presents Seppe with an occasion to hand him the magic tooth, for which he is to be amply rewarded. His most wonderful gift, however, is Vrone's love. And with this ending, Mörike diverges from most other fairy tales in which the heroes find happiness and wealth far away from home. The world he portrays in his tale thus appears more limited—it is at the same time more concrete and realistic. The same tendency can be observed throughout the tale. While folk fairy tales give indication of being abstractions by stressing a magic number (for example, by testing the hero three times), Mörike was carried away by his love for details and forgot all about the abstractions. The number three only plays a role in the three gifts of the Lau. Mörike also acquaints us with his characters much more closely than fairy tales, which usually stress only one trait. He weaves so many folklore elements into his story that it can be read as a chapter in a description of customs and manners in Swabia at the time of the famous Count Eberhard. The story is a glorification of the life and people in Swabia. Yet we should not understand it in too narrow a sense. Like the other fairy tales, it is also a mirror of the world, of its joys and troubles, of love and crime, trickery and generosity, life and death, good and evil.

In 1853, one year after "The Hutzelmännlein" was published, there appeared another, much shorter work from Mörike's pen, "Die Hand der Jezerte" (The Hand of Jezerte). He himself called it "a kind of fairy tale in archaic style."[45] What did he mean with the designation "archaic"? Did the work again describe the customs of earlier times like "The Hutzelmännlein"? Or was he referring not to content but to form? A look at the story may answer these questions.

At first glance, it seems that its protagonists resemble usual fairy tale figures much more than the simple Swabians in "The Hutzelmännlein." In this tale, a king falls in love with Jezerte, the daughter of his gardener. He marries her but she dies a year later. The king has a beautiful statue of his beloved erected in his garden, and once a month he goes there to pray. He does not eat or drink then because his heart is sick with longing for Jezerte. But he has a mistress, Naïra, who is jealous of the deceased. She calls a youth who loves her secretly, as she well knows, and asks him to break off a hand of the statue and to bring it to her. The young man is disturbed, however, in this undertaking, flees, and drops the hand in a bed of violets, where the king finds it the next morning. The youth is caught and thrown into jail. Naïra, in order to save him, advises him he should tell the king that Jezerte had loved him before she had met the king. To make his story more believable, the young man withstands torture for three days before he gives his secret away. The king lets him go but becomes very melancholy himself, because he must assume that Jezerte has been false to him.

He has the hand fastened in its old place and one night, when he cannot sleep, he goes to the temple to pray for a sign whether Jezerte was innocent. As soon as he asks this question, the entire room is filled with the fragrance of violets, and he feels sure that his love for Jezerte has been justified. He offers a reward to anyone who would find the guilty person, for he is certain that the youth has acted on someone's orders. The next morning Naïra does not come to him at the accustomed hour. When he surprises her in her room, he finds that her right hand has turned black like leather. He gives orders to send her away to a wild place.

His cousin, however, who has always hated her, takes her to a deserted island where she would not be able to survive. She sees through his intentions, yet does not complain and accepts her fate. Her only wish is that her hand might be clean again, and she asks the guards to bring her some water from Jezerte's well, hoping this will cure her if she asked Jezerte to forgive her. The men refuse, but when they are on their way home from the island, they observe the figure of another woman next to Naïra. And when the youth who loved her comes two days later to free her, he finds her dead and her hands both white. He goes to the king and tells him what has happened. They are sure that Jezerte has forgiven Naïra and they honor Naïra also by clearing the island and giving her a burial where they have found her. The cruel cousin is sent out of the country.

Upon learning of the content of this work, the reader must feel reminded of the usual folk fairy tales, probably more so than in the case of "The Hutzelmännlein." It is a tale of a king and his love, fair judgment, and his mistress' love and jealousy. The characters are types rather than persons with whom the reader would identify, as he does with Seppe and Vrone. It seems as if the story were not fixed in time or place and remained abstract like a paradigm. But upon a closer look, we notice motifs that do point to a certain historical period during the Middle Ages when Germanic, Christian, and Oriental beliefs and customs were fused. The motif of the ordeal, for example, although known to many Indo-European peoples, was elaborated upon by Christians and reflected in the literature of the time, as in Gottfried von Strassburg's *Tristan and Isolde*. The *Gesta Romanorum*,[46] a Latin collection of anecdotes and tales compiled in the late thirteenth or early fourteenth century, reflects the fusion of classical and oriental stories with Christian legends which must have been common property of people of the time. It abounds in motifs similar to the ones found in Mörike's story. We find there the jealousy of the second wife, we hear of speaking trees and magic wells and of statues emitting a sweet smell. Hands frequently figure as magic hands or hands which wither or change color, and also hands which are restored. While these motifs suggest the background of legal trials based on the belief in a divine judgment that can be revealed in ordeals, the end of Mörike's tale reminds us of legendary themes. Naïra and the people hold Jezerte in great esteem, as if she were a saint. On the other hand, the story of Jezerte is set in an atmosphere similar to that of Erinna in Mörike's poem "Erinna to Sappho." Both works describe the morning toiletries of the girls, mention precious oils and byssos web, details which, in Mörike's mind, must have constituted a certain classical flavor.

A glance at the dates of the conception and publication of the fairy tale affords us an explanation of this classical influence. The first draft of the beginning of the story accompanied a letter to Hartlaub in 1841, the year after the publication of the *Anthology of Classical Poetry*. Mörike completed the fairy tale in 1853, two years before he finished the translation of idylls by Theocritus for Notter's edition. The tale thus stems from a period in which he occupied himself intensely with the ancient tradition and wrote most of his poetry in classical meter. "Erinna to Sappho" was going to be a very late fruit of this harvest in 1863. By that time, the figure of the girl whom Death called from the joys of Youth had been transformed in the poet's mind from the beloved of a young king into a young poetess loved and mourned by the famous Sappho. Retaining the elements of the girl's pre-occupation with her appearance and her predilection for precious ointments and clothes, he had transformed her into a symbol of even deeper value by adding the gift of poetry to the themes of beauty and love. At the same time, he intensified his story by simplification when he omitted the array of characters sur-rounding Jezerte and the king and concentrated on the story of love and death, without distracting from it through a phase of doubt, as the one induced by Naïra in the tale of Jezerte.

The content of the story, then, is a combination of the classi-cal and medieval. Mörike's description of it as "archaic" is, therefore, justified. The tale is written in a highly stylized prose that is only one step removed from the free rhythm of "Erinna to Sappho." One can see this if he follows the beginning of the story:

Before the early light appeared in the king's garden, the leaves of the myrtle tree stirred and it said:

"I sense the morning wind in my branches; I am drinking sweet dew already: when will Jezerte come?"

And with a whisper the nut-pine answered:

"Already I see her through the graceful screen of the lower window, the gardener's youngest daughter. Soon she will step out of the house, climb down the steps to the well and bathe her face, the beautiful girl."

And the well replied:

"The dear child has no balm, no attar of roses; she dips her hair into my clear blackness, she draws my water with her hands. Hush! I hear the lovely girl come."

And the gardener's daughter came to the well, washed herself and combed and braided her hair.

And behold, it so happened that Athmas, the king, went forth from the palace to enjoy the morning-coolness before the coming of the day; he walked hither the wide path on yellow sand and noticed the girl, came closer and stopped in amazement because of her beauty; he greeted the frightened girl and kissed her forehead.

Since then she was dear to Athmas and stayed close to him day and night; she wore precious garments of byssos and silk and was honored by the king's cousins for she was loving and modest with the great and the humble; and she gave much to the poor.

After a year, however, Jezerte fell ill; no help was possible, and she died in her youth.

Then the king had a tomb built for her at the edge of the palace garden where the well sprang up; and above it a small temple, and he had her image placed in it made of white marble, showing her full figure as if alive, a miracle of the arts. And the people held the well sacred.[47]

The style of this tale appears somewhat forced, at times, when the reader becomes conscious of the fact that it is a combination of the naïve and simple tone of folk fairy tales and boasts a vocabularly that suggests a Southern or Middle Eastern setting. It is as precious as the style of the fairy tales written by Goethe and Novalis who wanted to reveal mythological content in highly select style. The tendency toward the oriental in Mörike's work, however, reminds us also of the style of Platen and Rückert, his contemporaries, whose scholarly knowledge of oriental literature was reflected in their own poetry. We know that Mörike considered their poetry stilted and unnatural. He may have applied the same criticism to "The Hand of Jezerte" and thus decided not to write any more in the same vein. The experiment with this style, however, still bore fruit in his later writings, when he employed some of its vocabulary in such works as "Erinna to Sappho."

CHAPTER 4

Conclusion: Mörike and His Readers Today

AFTER following the discussion of various aspects of Eduard Mörike's work, the reader of our time is likely to ask himself what he has gained from becoming acquainted with this nineteenth-century German poet. Indeed, he may have wondered whether Mörike's poetry—which is concerned with nature and such basic experiences as love and happiness, the relations between friends and relatives, the threat of death, and the demonic depth of the creative moment—can have much meaning to himself, whose problems seem to lie in other, apparently more complex spheres of human involvement of a social, political, or philosophical nature. What is it then that the more sophisticated reader can find in Mörike?

Before answering this question, we ought to look at the "sophisticated" reader himself and to describe his relationship to the world that surrounds him in more detail. It is true that he would quickly extract himself from some situations to which Mörike submitted. As a literary man, today's reader would not stay in small villages among farmers without any media to keep him in touch with intellectual developments. The reader of our time probes into new realms opened to us by the sciences and a deeper insight into the human psyche. He may expand his vision with the help of stimulants which far exceed the effect that natural phenomena or human relations had on Mörike, and he may be searching for new forms in which to express his experiences. But the complexity of his experiences weighs heavily on his mind; and when he returns from his exalted journeys into the dream world, or when he is tiring from his cerebral games with computers and from the hope of fighting the inequities of a society ruled by prejudices and inefficiency, he looks around for companionship, kindness, and simplicity which may calm his mind and his heart.

[143]

It is not a return to the primitive that he longs for, and he does not want to become part of some movement that promises to "save" him. What he needs is a reassurance of the wealth in his own heart presented in a form which stimulates his intellect.

Such wealth of the human heart, a certain richness even in suffering, and a basic courage to try this life over and over again is expressed in Mörike's works in a most sophisticated form. It is expressed in words and images which are timeless. For what we have called the romantic elements in his works, or his *Biedermeier* tendencies, are characteristics which any period contains to a certain degree. In Mörike's finest works they are never exaggerated to an extent that would make them interesting only to literary historians. Even in his expressions of extreme grief or exaltation, Mörike practiced restraint, which raises his poetry to that level of literature which permits us to read the works of the ancients as if they were written for us today. The manner of restraint, so we noticed, was mainly form, which Mörike applied so masterfully to his content as to give many of his poems an excellence which we have called classical—but not merely because some of the forms stem from classical antiquity. Even a poem like "Erinna to Sappho," where classical meter just barely shines through the free rhythm, or a novella like "Mozart on the Way to Prague," with its loose composition of frame story and inserted episodes, do not interfere with our notion of the classical Mörike because we feel that these works adhere to an inner discipline, which stems from the poet's submission to his task. Such discipline, as well as the artistic accomplishment, may be less obvious in Mörike's works than in those of other writers, simply because they are veiled in gracefulness and charm in his idyllic poetry, or penetrated by the direct expression of joy or sorrow, exaltation or anxiety, in the early nature poems and those of the Peregrina cycle. In these poems, content seems to prevail over form. They touch our emotions directly because the poet himself appears to have been more strongly overcome by his experiences than in the later poetry, in which humor often is an indication of the mastery of a situation. But poems like those of the Peregrina cycle or "On a Winter Morning" also move us so deeply because they express our own longings for love and fulfillment.

[144]

Conclusion: Mörike and His Readers Today

Besides Mörike's works of universal appeal and timeless beauty, we have also analyzed those of his writings which are of a more limited interest to the present-day reader. *Nolten the Painter* can be considered as an interesting study in psychological phenomena and in the problem of man's freedom of will, interspersed with descriptions of life in different strata of society and with discussions of the problems of the artist. Mörike's fairy tales, with their wealth of motifs and their rather realistic insights into human nature, can still charm the modern reader. Some of his poems will still entertain children and audiences who enjoy a humorous story. A phantasmagoria like that of the last king of Orplid is as relevant as many a modern attempt to depict the problem of Time.

The modern reader, therefore, may very well find the warmth of heart and the courage to face this world in the works of a man who seemed to withdraw from the "wide wide world," but who in his poetry reflected deep and intense experiences of life's joys and sorrows. Being more sensitive than most men, he did not need to see much of the world in order to know of its essence and to transform it into works of enduring significance.

Notes and References

Chapter One

1. Quoted in S. S. Prawer, *Mörike und seine Leser* (Stuttgart, 1960), p. 17.
2. *Mörikes Werke*, ed. H. Maync, 2nd ed., 3 vols. (Leipzig and Vienna, 1914), III, 385 f. The fragment is a humorous account of a night which the student Spillner has to spend in detention.
3. The irregularity in the use of tenses is found in the manuscript. There are two studies of Mörike's creative process: L. Dieckmann, "Mörike's Presentation of the Creative Process," *Journal of English and Germanic Philology*, LIII (1954), 291–305 and H. Slessarev, "Der Abgrund der Betrachtung. Über den schöpferischen Vorgang bei Mörike," *German Quarterly*, XXXIV (1961), 41–49.
4. Eduard Mörike, *Briefe*, ed. F. Seebaß (Tübingen, 1939), p. 44.
5. Quoted in A. Beck, "Peregrina," *Euphorion*, XLVII (1953), 214.
6. *Briefe*, p. 433f.
7. *Ibid.*, p. 105.
8. *Ibid.*, p. 133.
9. *Ibid.*, p. 212.
10. *Ibid.*, p. 374.
11. *Ibid.*, p. 136. In a letter of Sept. 27, 1830, he stated that he was reading the correspondence for the fifth time already. See *Briefe*, p. 247.
12. *Ibid.*, p. 432f.
13. M. Mare, *Eduard Mörike: The Man and the Poet* (London, 1957), p. 156. She follows B. v. Wiese, *Eduard Mörike* (Tübingen and Stuttgart, 1950), p. 55.
14. R. Wellek and A. Warren, *Theory of Literature*, 2nd ed. (New York: Harvest Books, 1956), p. 75, mention the idiosyncrasies of a few other authors.
15. In his letters of 1847, he describes his condition as a weakness of the spine and dates his poor state of health as far back as 1835. See *Briefe*, pp. 634 and 643.
16. In December 1840, he had set up an altar in his house, which his mother found "beautiful, but Catholic!" See *Briefe*, p. 507.
17. *Ibid.*, pp. 781 and 758, respectively.

18. H. H. Krummacher, "Zu Mörikes Gedichten," *Jahrbuch der Deutschen Schillergesellschaft,* V (1961), 340.

19. *Briefe,* p. 733.

20. He had followed the patriotic attempts to create a more liberal constitution for Germany in 1848 with similar enthusiasm. See *Briefe,* p. 650f.

21. A much more extensive account of the poet's life is given in H. Maync, *Eduard Mörike,* 3rd and 4th eds. (Stuttgart and Berlin, 1927).

Chapter Two

1. For the changes in the understanding and classification of Mörike's poetry see the very thorough study by S. S. Prawer, *Mörike und seine Leser* (Stuttgart, 1960).

2. A. Beck in his interpretation of the poem "An einem Wintermorgen, vor Sonnenaufgang," *Euphorion,* XLVI (1952), 388.

3. B. v. Wiese, *Eduard Mörike* (Tübingen and Stuttgart, 1950), p. 99.

4.

Im Park

Sieh, der Kastanie kindliches Laub hängt noch wie der feuchte
    Flügel des Papillons, wenn er die Hülle verließ;
Aber in laulicher Nacht der kürzeste Regen entfaltet
    Leise die Fächer und deckt schnell den luftigen Gang.
—Du magst eilen, o himmlischer Frühling, oder verweilen,
    Immer dem trunkenen Sinn fliehst du, ein Wunder, vorbei.

Poems are quoted according to the edition of *Mörikes Werke* by H. Maync. For lack of space only a few German versions could be included in these footnotes. Emphasis will be on those poems of which specific phrases or motifs are analyzed in the text. See also the interpretation of the poem by F. Lösel in *Wirkendes Wort,* XII (1962), 155–61.

5. See Krummacher, "Mitteilungen zur Chronologie und Textgeschichte von Mörikes Gedichten," *Jb. d. Schillerges.,* VI (1962), 259, for the date.

6.

Die schöne Buche

Ganz verborgen im Wald kenn' ich ein Plätzchen, da stehet
    Eine Buche, man sieht schöner im Bilde sie nicht.
Rein und glatt, in gediegenem Wuchs erhebt sie sich einzeln,
    Keiner der Nachbarn rührt ihr an dem seidenen Schmuck.
Rings, so weit sein Gezweig' der stattliche Baum ausbreitet,
    Grünet der Rasen, das Aug' still zu erquicken, umher;
Gleich nach allen Seiten umzirkt er den Stamm in der Mitte;
    Kunstlos schuf die Natur selber dies liebliche Rund.
Zartes Gebüsch umkränzet es erst; hochstämmige Bäume,
    Folgend in dichtem Gedräng', wehren dem himmlischen Blau.

Neben der dunkleren Fülle des Eichbaums wieget die Birke
Ihr jungfräuliches Haupt schüchtern im goldenen Licht.
Nur wo, verdeckt vom Felsen, der Fußsteig jäh sich hinabschlingt,
Lässet die Hellung mich ahnen das offene Feld.
—Als ich unlängst einsam, von neuen Gestalten des Sommers
Ab dem Pfade gelockt, dort im Gebüsch mich verlor,
Führt' ein freundlicher Geist, des Hains auflauschende Gottheit,
Hier mich zum erstenmal, plötzlich, den Staunenden, ein.
Welch Entzücken! Es war um die hohe Stunde des Mittags,
Lautlos alles, es schwieg selber der Vogel im Laub.
Und ich zauderte noch, auf den zierlichen Teppich zu treten;
Festlich empfing er den Fuß, leise beschritt ich ihn nur.
Jetzo, gelehnt an den Stamm (er trägt sein breites Gewölbe
nicht zu hoch), ließ ich rundum die Augen ergehn,
Wo den beschatteten Kreis die feurig strahlende Sonne,
Fast gleich messend umher, säumte mit blendendem Rand.
Aber ich stand und rührte mich nicht; dämonischer Stille,
Unergründlicher Ruh' lauschte mein innerer Sinn.
Eingeschlossen mit *dir* in diesem sonnigen Zauber-
Gürtel, o *Einsamkeit*, fühlt' ich und dachte nur dich!

The Italics in the concluding lines are mine. There is a careful interpretation
of this poem by Romano Guardini in *Gegenwart und Geheimnis* (Würzburg,
1957), pp. 15–24.

7. W. v. Nordheim, "Die Einsamkeitserfahrung Mörikes und ihre
Aussprache im dichterischen Werk" Diss. [Hamburg, 1954] deals with
the various shades of Mörike's experience of solitude and loneliness.

8. See Krummacher, *Jb. d. Schillerges.*, VI (1962), 261 and 288–90
for the genesis of this poem.

9. Krummacher, *Jb. d. Schillerges.*, V (1961), 324–25 and 337–41.

10. For the shifting of motifs and an interpretation of the poem see
J. C. Middleton, "Mörike's Moonchild," *Publ. of the English Goethe
Society*, N. S. 28 (1959), 109–28.

11. *Briefe*, p. 140.

12.   *An eine Äolsharfe*
Tu semper urges flebilibus modis
Mystem ademptum: nec tibi Vesper
Surgente decedunt amores,
          Nec rapidum fugiente Solem.
                              Horaz

          Angelehnt an die Efeuwand
Dieser alten Terrasse,
Du, einer luftgebornen Muse
Geheimnisvolles Saitenspiel,
Fang an,
Fange wieder an
Deine melodische Klage!

Ihr kommet, Winde, fern herüber,
Ach! von des Knaben,
Der mir so lieb war,
Frisch grünendem Hügel.
Und Frühlingsblüten unterweges streifend,
Übersättigt mit Wohlgerüchen,
Wie süß bedrängt ihr dies Herz!
Und säuselt her in die Saiten,
Angezogen von wohllautender Wehmut,
Wachsend im Zug meiner Sehnsucht,
Und hinsterbend wieder.

Aber auf einmal,
Wie der Wind heftiger herstößt,
Ein holder Schrei der Harfe
Wiederholt, mir zu süßem Erschrecken,
Meiner Seele plötzliche Regung;
Und hier—die volle Rose streut, geschüttelt,
All ihre Blätter vor meine Füße!

13. W. Höllerer, *Zwischen Klassik und Moderne* (Stuttgart, 1958),
p. 330.

14. *Ibid.*, p. 334.

15. See his remarks about the double activity of the soul in: *Werke,*
II, 483.

16. Krummacher, *Jb. d. Schillerges.*, VI (1962), 309.

17.   O, hier ist's, wo Natur den Schleier reißt!
Sie bricht einmal ihr übermenschlich Schweigen;
Laut mit sich selber redend, will ihr Geist,
Sich selbst vernehmend, sich ihm selber zeigen.

18. *Briefe,* p. 358.

19.   An einem Wintermorgen, vor Sonnenaufgang

O flaumenleichte Zeit der dunkeln Frühe!
Welch neue Welt bewegest du in mir?
Was ist's, daß ich auf einmal nun in dir
Von sanfter Wollust meines Daseins glühe?

Einem Krystall gleicht meine Seele nun,
Den noch kein falscher Strahl des Lichts getroffen;
Zu fluten scheint mein Geist, er scheint zu ruhn,
Dem Eindruck naher Wunderkräfte offen,
Die aus dem klaren Gürtel blauer Luft
Zuletzt ein Zauberwort vor meine Sinne ruft.

Bei hellen Augen glaub' ich doch zu schwanken;
Ich schließe sie, daß nicht der Traum entweiche.
Seh' ich hinab in lichte Feenreiche?
Wer hat den bunten Schwarm von Bildern und Gedanken

Zur Pforte meines Herzens hergeladen,
Die glänzend sich in diesem Busen baden,
Goldfarb'gen Fischlein gleich im Gartentciche?

Ich höre bald der Hirtenflöte Klänge,
Wie um die Krippe jener Wundernacht,
Bald weinbekränzter Jugend Lustgesänge;
Wer hat das friedenselige Gedränge
In meine traurigen Wände hergebracht?

Und welch Gefühl entzückter Stärke,
Indem mein Sinn sich frisch zur Ferne lenkt!
Vom ersten Mark des heut'gen Tags getränkt,
Fühl ich mir Mut zu jedem frommen Werke.
Die Seele fliegt, soweit der Himmel reicht,
Der Genius jauchzt in mir! Doch sage,
Warum wird jetzt der Blick von Wehmut feucht?
Ist's ein verloren Glück, was mich erweicht?
Ist es ein werdendes, was ich im Herzen trage?
—Hinweg, mein Geist! hier gilt kein Stillestehn:
Es ist ein Augenblick, und alles wird verwehn!

Dort, sieh! am Horizont lüpft sich der Vorhang schon!
Es träumt der Tag, nun sei die Nacht entflohn;
Die Purpurlippe, die geschlossen lag,
Haucht, hell geöffnet, süße, Atemzüge:
Auf einmal blitzt das Aug, und, wie ein Gott, der Tag
Beginnt im Sprung die königlichen Flüge!

20. E. Staiger, *Die Zeit als Einbildungskraft des Dichters* (Zurich, 1939).

21. E. Staiger, "Mörike: 'Das verlassene Mägdlein,'" *Trivium*, V (1947), 44–53.

22. W. Kohlschmidt, "Wehmut, Erinnerung, Sehnsucht in Mörikes Gedicht," *Wirkendes Wort*, I (1950–51), 229–38, particularly 232f.; reprinted in *Form und Innerlichkeit* (Bern, 1955).

23. Beck in *Euphorion*, XLVI (1952), 370–93.

24. *Ibid.*, p. 389.

25. Prawer, *op. cit.*, p. 113.

26. Beck in *Euphorion*, XLVI (1952), 374–75.

27. *Ibid.*, p. 198.

28. For the relationship of the poems "At Night" and "Song of Two at Night" and *Spillner* see Krummacher, *Jb. d. Schillerges.*, V (1961), 314, n.

29.   Gesang zu zweien in der Nacht
    Sie: Wie süß der Nachtwind nun die Wiese streift
         Und klingend jetzt den jungen Hain durchläuft!

Da noch der freche Tag verstummt,
Hört man der Erdenkräfte flüsterndes Gedränge,
Das aufwärts in die zärtlichen Gesänge,
Der reingestimmten Lüfte summt.

Er: Vernehm' ich doch die wunderbarsten Stimmen,
Vom lauen Wind wollüstig hingeschleift,
Indes, mit ungewissem Licht gestreift,
Der Himmel selber scheinet hinzuschwimmen.

Sie: Wie ein Gewebe zuckt die Luft manchmal,
Durchsichtiger und heller aufzuwehen;
Dazwischen hört man weiche Töne gehen
Von sel'gen Feen, die im blauen Saal
Zum Sphärenklang,
Und fleißig mit Gesang,
Silberne Spindeln hin und wieder drehen.

Er. O holde Nacht, du gehst mit leisem Tritt
Auf schwarzem Samt, der nur am Tage grünet,
Und luftig schwirrender Musik bedienet
Sich nun dein Fuß zum leichten Schritt,
Womit du Stund' um Stunde missest,
Dich lieblich in dir selbst vergissest—
Du schwärmst, es schwärmt der Schöpfung Seele mit!

30. For the date see Krummacher, *Jb. d. Schillerges.*, VI (1962), 258.

31. Krummacher discusses Mörike's work on this poem in *Jb. d. Schillerges.*, VI (1962), 281ff. There had been three earlier versions of the poem. The second contained a "motif from the past" which Mörike later consciously eliminated. The motif had shown the evil Margaret—the personification of the wind—and her helpers to be the destroyers of the prince's castle and thus the instigators of his wanderings. For the respective stanzas see Maync, *Werke*, I, 458f.

32. R. Ibel, *Weltschau deutscher Dichter*, II (Hamburg, 1948), 111. G. Storz, *Eduard Mörike* (Stuttgart, 1967), p. 273, feels that the new stanza is consistent with the earlier ones in which the fire-rider was also depicted as a sorcerer who could frivolously use a piece of the holy cross to ban the fire.

33.   Schön-Rohtraut
Wie heißt König Ringangs Töchterlein?
Rohtraut, Schön-Rohtraut.
Was tut sie denn den ganzen Tag,
Da sie wohl nicht spinnen und nähen mag?
Tut fischen und jagen.
O daß ich doch ihr Jäger wär'!

Fischen und Jagen freute mich sehr.
—Schweig stille, mein Herze!

Und über eine kleine Weil',
   Rohtraut, Schön-Rohtraut,
So dient der Knab' auf Ringangs Schloß
In Jägertracht und hat ein Roß,
   Mit Rohtraut zu jagen.
O daß ich doch ein Königssohn wär'!
Rohtraut, Schön-Rohtraut lieb ich so sehr.
—Schweig stille, mein Herze!

Einsmals sie ruhten am Eichenbaum,
   Da lacht Schön-Rohtraut:
"Was siehst mich an so wunniglich?
Wenn du das Herz hast, küsse mich!"
   Ach! erschrak der Knabe!
Doch denket er: "Mir ist's vergunnt",
Und küsset Schön-Rohtraut auf den Mund.
—Schweig stille, mein Herze!

Darauf sie ritten schweigend heim,
   Rohtraut, Schön-Rohtraut;
Es jauchzt der Knab' in seinem Sinn:
"Und würdst du heute Kaiserin,
   Mich sollt's nicht kränken!
Ihr tausend Blätter im Walde wißt,
Ich hab' Schön-Rohtrauts Mund geküßt!
—Schweig stille, mein Herze!"

34. *Briefe,* p. 831.
35. *Ibid.,* pp. 430ff.
36.   Das verlassene Mägdlein
    Früh, wann die Hähne krähn,
    Eh' die Sternlein verschwinden,
    Muß ich am Herde stehn,
    Muß Feuer zünden.

    Schön ist der Flammen Schein,
    Es springen die Funken;
    Ich schaue so drein,
    In Leid versunken.

    Plötzlich, da kommt es mir,
    Treuloser Knabe,
    Daß ich die Nacht von dir
    Geträumet habe.

    Träne auf Träne dann
    Stürzet hernieder;
    So kommt der Tag heran—
    O ging' er wieder!

See the interpretation of this poem by E. Staiger, "Mörike: Das verlassene Mägdlein," *Trivium*, V (Zurich, 1947), 44–53, and again in *Die Kunst der Interpretation* (Zurich, 1955), pp. 205–14.

37. See W. Taraba, "Eduard Mörike: 'Denk' es, o Seele!'" in *Die deutsche Lyrik*, ed. B. v. Wiese (Düsseldorf, 1957), II, 91–97.

38. Beck, *Euphorion*, XLVII (1953), 206–7.

39. Peregrina III

Ein Irrsal kam in die Mondscheingärten
Einer einst heiligen Liebe.
Schaudernd entdeckt' ich verjährten Betrug.
Und mit weinendem Blick, doch grausam,
Hieß ich das schlanke,
Zauberhafte Mädchen
Ferne gehen von mir.
Ach, ihre hohe Stirn
War gesenkt, denn sie liebte mich;
Aber sie zog mit Schweigen
Fort in die graue
Welt hinaus.

Krank seitdem,
Wund ist und wehe mein Herz.
Nimmer wird es genesen!

Als ginge, luftgesponnen, ein Zauberfaden
Von ihr zu mir, ein ängstig Band,
So zieht es, zieht mich schmachtend ihr nach!
—Wie? wenn ich eines Tages auf meiner Schwelle
Sie sitzen fände, wie einst, im Morgen-Zwielicht,
Das Wanderbündel neben ihr,
Und ihr Auge, treuherzig zu mir aufschauend,
Sagte, da bin ich wieder
Hergekommen aus weiter Welt!

40. See Beck, *Euphorion*, XLVII (1953), 213 for the symbolism of "house" and "world."

41. *Ibid.*, pp. 208–9.

42. For the unpublished stanza of 'Peregrina I' see *Werke*, I, 467:
Einst ließ ein Traum von wunderbarem Leben
Mich sprießend Gold in tiefer Erde seh'n,
Geheime Lebens-Kräfte, die da weben
In dunkeln Schachten, ahnungsvoll verstehn;
Mich drang's hinab, nicht konnt' ich widerstreben,
Und unten, wie verzweifelt, blieb ich stehn,—
Die goldnen Adern konnt' ich nirgend schauen,
Und um mich schüttert sehnsuchtvolles Grauen.

43. Beck in *Euphorion*, XLVII (1953), 212.

44. *Ibid.*, p. 200.

45. The manuscript version is quoted *Ibid.*, p. 201.
46. The early version can be found in *Werke*, I, 467:
> Und nun strich sie mir, stille stehend,
> Seltsamen Blicks mit dem Finger die Schläfe,
> Jählings versank ich in tiefen Schlummer,
> Aber gestärkt vom Wunderschlafe
> Bin ich erwacht zu glückseligen Tagen,
> Führte die seltsame Braut in mein Haus ein.

47. Storz, pp. 118ff. stresses the difference in the intellectual and cultural climate in Catholic Upper Swabia as compared with that of the almost Puritan Old Württemberg from where Mörike came. According to him Mörike could feel freed here from inhibitions regarding erotic experiences as well as artistic ones. He even joined a theater group one day for a performance of Schiller's "Love and Intrigue." It was this atmosphere as much as any one experience with a particular girl that inspired the love poetry of 1828. Many of these poems, especially, however, "Predictions of Love" and the short poem "Josephine" are so close to the rococo poetry of the eighteenth century that the reader may wonder whether Mörike's reading at the time was influential also.

It might also be noted here that Storz, p. 120, takes issue with Maync's assertion that Mörike's love in Scheer was the daughter of the schoolteacher. He does not find enough support for this statement. In her book *Eduard Mörike: The Man and the Poet*, pp. 196f., M. Mare bases the discussion of Mörike's sexual inclinations on an interpretation of his drawings, mainly those which he sent as gifts to Hartlaub's children: a drawing of Adam's coat-of-arms, for example, with a gray wraith, from the head of which a snake emerges behind a big red figleaf, on which is superimposed a black fruit; or one of a man holding his entrails; or that of a devil using his long tail to fire off a cannon. These and several other drawings are all called obscene. A psychiatrist is quoted as having found that Mörike was emotionally fixed at an early stage, afraid of life and unable to meet its demands. These findings seem to have little bearing on his poetry, though, and should not stand in the way of those who want to read the poems unburdened by biographical details.

48. These lines are a rather free translation of the last stanza of "Nimmersatte Liebe":
> So ist die Lieb'! und war auch so,
> Wie lang' es Liebe gibt,
> Und anders war Herr Salomo,
> Der Weise nicht verliebt.

49. For the date see Krummacher, *Jb. d. Schillerges.*, VI (1962), 259.

50. Only the last lines are translated; the ones before are a rather free rendering of a part of the poem "Götterwink":
..., hinter dem nächtlichen Fenster, bewegt sich
Plötzlich, wie Fackelschein, eilig vorüber ein Licht,
Stark herstrahlend zu mir, und hebt aus dem dunkeln Gebüsche
Dicht mir zur Seite die hoch glühende Rose hervor.
Heil! o Blume, du willst mir verkünden, o götterberührte,
Welche Wonne noch heut mein, des Verwegenen, harrt
Im verschloßnen Gemach. Wie schlägt mein Busen!—Erschütternd
Ist der Dämonien Ruf, auch der den Sieg dir verspricht.

51. Höllerer, *op. cit.*, p. 356, points to the ambiguity of the word "aufbricht" (breaks up). It may also indicate that the deeper meaning of church becomes apparent.

52. These are the two tercets of the poem "Am Walde":
Und wenn die feinen Leute nur erst dächten,
Wie schön Poeten ihre Zeit verschwenden,
Sie würden mich zuletzt noch gar beneiden.

Denn des Sonetts gedrängte Kränze flechten
Sich wie von selber unter meinen Händen,
Indes die Augen in der Ferne weiden.

53. *Briefe*, p. xviii.

54. A modern edition of Mörike's translations appeared in two volumes in the Sammlung Klosterberg: *Römische Lyrik* (Basel, 1946) and *Griechische Lyrik* (Basel, 1949).

55. About the value of his translations see Gerda Rupprecht, "Mörikes Leistung als Übersetzer aus den klassischen Sprachen," Diss. (Munich, 1958).

56. R. B. Farrell, "Mörike's Classical Verse," *Publ. of the English Goethe Society*, N. S. 25 (1956), p. 52, points to the kinship between Mörike and these two poets of antiquity.

57. See the letter of Dec. 10, 1831.

58. Auf eine Lampe
Noch unverrückt, o schöne Lampe, schmückest du,
An leichten Ketten zierlich aufgehangen hier,
Die Decke des nun fast vergessnen Lustgemachs.
Auf deiner weißen Marmorschale, deren Rand
Der Efeukranz von goldengrünem Erz umflicht,
Schlingt fröhlich eine Kinderschar den Ringelreih'n.
Wie reizend alles! lachend, und ein sanfter Geist
Des Ernstes doch ergossen um die ganze Form—
Ein Kunstgebild' der echten Art. Wer achtet sein?
Was aber schön ist, selig scheint es in ihm selbst.

59. See: M. Heidegger/E. Staiger, "Zu einem Vers von Mörike," *Trivium*, IX (1951), 1–16.

Notes and References

60. I. Appelbaum-Graham, "Zu Mörikes Gedicht 'Auf eine Lampe'," *Modern Language Notes,* LXVIII (1953), 328–34.

61. W. v. Nordheim, "Die Dingdichtung Eduard Mörikes," *Euphorion,* L (1956), 71–85, also makes this suggestion.

62. Quoted in Krummacher, *Jb. d. Schillerges.,* V (1961), 339.

63. Farrell, *op. cit.,* p. 53 quotes a few lines from Tibullus which express the same wish.

64. *Werke,* I, 442. Maync gives several examples.

65. Ulrich Hötzer, " 'Grata Negligentia'—'Ungestiefelte Hexameter'? Bemerkungen zu Goethes und Mörikes Hexameter" in: *Der Deutschunterricht,* vol. 16 (1964) pp. 99f. praises the use Mörike made of the hexameter. Especially the revisions of the poem on the "Trusty Man" and "The Idyl from Lake Constance" indicate that he wanted to follow the classical rules for this meter. He does avail himself, however, of any "exceptions" within the established usage and thus brings a spondee in the fifth foot or words with a double accent at the end of the line. He thus obtains a greater flexibility in this meter than even Goethe or Voß had done.

66. *Briefe,* p. 123.

67. See Krummacher, *Jb. d. Schillerges.,* VI (1962), 262ff., for the dates of origin of the cycle.

68.   Erinna an Sappho

"Vielfach sind zum Hades die Pfade", heißt ein
Altes Liedchen—"und einen gehst du selber,
Zweifle nicht!" Wer, süßeste Sappho, zweifelt?
Sagt es nicht jeglicher Tag?
Doch den Lebenden haftet nur leicht im Busen
Solch ein Wort, und dem Meer anwohnend ein Fischer von Kind auf
Hört im stumpferen Ohr der Wogen Geräusch nicht mehr.
—Wundersam aber erschrak mir heute das Herz. Vernimm!

Sonniger Morgenglanz im Garten,
Ergossen um der Bäume Wipfel,
Lockte die Langschläferin (denn so schaltest du jüngst Erinna!)
Früh vom schwüligen Lager hinweg.
Stille war mein Gemüt; in den Adern aber
Unstet klopfte das Blut bei der Wangen Blässe.

Als ich am Putztisch jetzo die Flechten löste,
Dann mit nardeduftendem Kamm vor der Stirn den Haar-
Schleier teilte,—seltsam betraf mich im Spiegel Blick in Blick.
Augen, sagt' ich, ihr Augen, was wollt ihr?
Du, mein Geist, heute noch sicher behaust da drinne,
Lebendigen Sinnen traulich vermählt,
Wie mit fremdendem Ernst, lächelnd halb, ein Dämon,

Nickst du mich an, Tod weissagend!
—Ha, da mit eins durchzuckt' es mich
Wie Wetterschein! wie wenn schwarzgefiedert ein tödlicher Pfeil
Streifte die Schläfe hart vorbei,
Daß ich, die Hände gedeckt aufs Antlitz, lange
Staunend blieb, in die nachtschaurige Kluft schwindelnd hinab.

Und das eigene Todesgeschick erwog ich;
Trockenen Aug's noch erst,
Bis da ich dein, o Sappho, dachte
Und der Freundinnen all
Und anmutiger Musenkunst,
Gleich da quollen die Tränen mir.

Und dort blinkte vom Tisch das schöne Kopfnetz, dein Geschenk,
Köstliches Byssosgeweb', von goldnen Bienlein schwärmend.
Dieses, wenn wir demnächst das blumige Fest
Feiern der herrlichen Tochter Demeters,
Möcht' ich i h r weihn, für meinen Teil und deinen;
Daß sie hold uns bleibe (denn viel vermag sie),
Daß du zu früh dir nicht die braune Locke mögest
Für Erinna vom lieben Haupte trennen.

69. Höllerer, *op. cit.*, pp. 343ff.
70. See his letter of March 27, 1888, quoted in H. Kneisel, "Mörike and Music," Diss. (Columbia University, 1949) p. 69.
71. See Kneisel, *op. cit.*, pp. 72ff., and Prawer, *Mörike und seine Leser,* pp. 35ff.
72. For the discussion of musical elements in Mörike's poetry see Kneisel, *op. cit.*, pp. 87ff.
73. *Ibid.*, p. 209.

Chapter Three

1. Beck, *Euphorion,* XLVII (1953), 216.
2. *Werke,* II, 200.
3. *Werke,* II, 231.
4. Mörike asked the psychiatrist Zeller to read the novel and was told that the psychological development, especially of Nolten's fiancée Agnes, was correct. *Briefe,* p. 306.
5. See S. S. Prawer, "Mignon's Revenge, A Study of Mörike's *Maler Nolten*," *Publ. of the English Goethe Society,* N. S. 25 (1956), 63ff.
6. Nolten's paintings remind one of the early poetry of his author, especially the Peregrina poems.

Notes and References

7. *Werke*, II, 235–36.

8. The phantasmagoria "Orplid" was discussed on pp. 46–47 of this study as an example of Mörike's gift to create myths and as an indication of his experience of time.

9. In 1833 he wrote that he was longing for a "healthy ideal subject that would assimilate an ancient form" as a counterweight to the morbid and woebegone literature of his time. *Briefe*, p. 397. But as early as 1829, when he was working on *Nolten*, he explained that he wanted to rid himself once and for all of this subjective material by writing it down. *Ibid.*, p. 140.

10. For a discussion of the role of fate and time see W. Taraba, "Die Rolle der Zeit und des Schicksals in Mörikes *Maler Nolten*," *Euphorion*, L (1956), 405–27.

11. See Prawer, *Publ. of the English Goethe Society*, p. 77.

12. *Ibid.*, p. 81.

13. *Werke*, II, 280.

14. *Werke*, II, 346.

15. The labyrinth, as well as the grotto in which Nolten embraces the Countess, are symbolic of his inner states and his groping for meaning in life.

16. B. v. Wiese elaborates on this relationship of the individual's fate to that of other family members on p. 178 of his study.

17. Beck, *Euphorion*, XLVII (1953), 215 and 217, wonders whether Mörike felt that in Elisabeth Nolten had betrayed his calling and thus had been disloyal to himself.

17a. Storz, 137, takes a completely new attitude in this respect. He considers the second edition to be a better reflection of the poet's intentions. He indicates his indebtedness for the reevaluation to the edition of G. Baumann who printed both versions and to the following article by Herbert Meyer: H. Meyer, "Stufen der Umgestaltung des Maler Nolten," in: *Zeitschrift für Deutsche Philologie*, vol. 85 (1966). In the meantime two volumes of the critical edition have appeared, volumes 3 and 4, containing *Nolten the Painter* and its revisions.

18. "Im Herbst des Jahres 1787 unternahm Mozart in Begleitung seiner Frau eine Reise nach Prag, um *Don Juan* daselbst zur Aufführung zu bringen. Am dritten Reisetag, den vierzehnten September, gegen elf Uhr morgens fuhr das wohlgelaunte Ehepaar, noch nicht viel über dreißig Stunden Wegs von Wien entfernt, in nordwestlicher Richtung jenseits vom Mannhardsberg und der deutschen Thaya bei Schrems, wo man das schöne Mährische Gebirg' bald vollends überstiegen hat." *Werke*, III, 213.

19. *Werke*, III, 218f.

20. *Werke*, III, 219f.

21. For the balance of melancholy and gaiety in this work see F. H. Mautner, *Mörikes "Mozart auf der Reise nach Prag"* (Krefeld, 1957).

22. *Werke*, III, 228f.

23. For the use of expressions like "suddenly" or "at once" in Mörike's work see H. Slessarev, "Der Abgrund der Betrachtung: Über den schöpferischen Vorgang bei Mörike." in *German Quarterly*, XXXIV (1961), 44f.

24. For example: K. Adrian, "Wege der Gestaltung in Mörikes *Maler Nolten* und 'Mozart auf der Reise nach Prag,' " Diss. (Münster, 1914). M. Ittenbach, "Mozart auf der Reise nach Prag," *GRM*, XXV (1937), 338–54. K. K. Polheim, "Der künstlerische Aufbau von Mörikes Mozartnovelle," *Euphorion*, XLVIII (1954), 41–70. Pp. 42–49 review all previous attempts at explaining the structure of the work. B. v. Wiese, "Eduard Mörike; 'Mozart auf der Reise nach Prag'," *Die deutsche Novelle* (Düsseldorf, 1960), pp. 213–37. F. H. Mautner, *Mörikes "Mozart auf der Reise nach Prag"* (Krefeld, 1957). R. B. Farrell, *Mörikes Mozart auf der Reise nach Prag* (London, 1960). R. Immerwahr, "Narrative and 'Musical' Structure in 'Mozart auf der Reise nach Prag'," *Studies in Germanic Languages and Literatures in Memory of Fred O. Nolte,* ed. E. Hofacker and L. Dieckmann (St. Louis, 1963), pp. 103–20.

25. Polheim, *op. cit.*, p. 51.

26. Farrell, *op. cit.*, p. 29.

27. For these attempts see Ittenbach and Immerwahr above.

28. Immerwahr, *op. cit.*, p. 120.

29. See R. Immerwahr, "Apocalyptic Trumpets: The Inception of 'Mozart auf der Reise nach Prag'," *PMLA*, LXX (1955), 390–407.

30. *Werke*, III, 269f.

31. *Werke*, III, 270f.

32. See R. Immerwahr's Essay (Note 29 above) for the trumpets and the connotations of "icy-cold" in Mörike's experience.

33. See Immerwahr, "Narrative and Musical Structure . . . ," p. 117.

34. *Werke*, III, 271.

35. The part now discussed is set off from the main narration of Mozart's stay at the castle. In this additional part the von Schinzbergs are again alone in their castle contemplating the impressions they gained from the encounter with the great composer. This may decrease the weight of Eugenia's fears. It is interesting that Mörike himself thought he was trying to show Mozart's gay side. *Briefe*, p. 730.

36. *Werke*, III, 275.

37. See the discussion of the poem on p. 56 above.

38. The Rococo background of Mozart and Mörike's careful description of its elements are discussed in the fine interpretation of the novella by F. H. Mautner, *Mörikes "Mozart auf der Reise nach Prag"* (Krefeld, 1957).

39. *Werke* III, 24f.

40. *Ibid.*, p. 294.

41. *Ibid.*, p. 38.

42. See H. Landmann, "Mörike's Märchen 'Das Stuttgarter Hutzelmännlein' im Verhältnis zum Volksmärchen," Diss. (Berlin, 1961) for the relationship of Mörike's tale to folk fairy tales.

43. See his letters to Storm and Hartlaub, *Briefe*, pp. 726 and 767, respectively.

44. *Werke*, III, 175.

45. *Briefe*, p. 733.

46. For this reference I am indebted to Eva Fleck who supplied me with a list of motifs found in Mörike's tale which occur repeatedly in the *Gesta Romanorum*. Most important may be the prevalence of an atmosphere mixed of ancient imagery and motifs from Christian legends. This similarity justifies Mörike's description "archaic" or "ancient."

47. *Werke*, III, 105.

Selected Bibliography

(a) The most important editions of Mörike's works and letters:

Mörikes Werke. Ed. H. Maync, 2nd ed., 3 vols. (Leipzig and Vienna, 1914). This has been the standard edition. It will be replaced during the coming years by a new critical edition, which is being prepared at the Mörike Archive in Marbach.

Eduard Mörikes sämtliche Werke. Ed. R. Krauß, 6 parts in 2 vols. (Leipzig, 1905). Contains some valuable hints and sources not given in Maync. The same is true of:

Mörikes Werke. Ed. K. Fischer, 6 vols. (Munich, 1906-08), which is not always reliable.

Mörikes Werke. Ed. A. Leffson, 4 parts in 2 vols. (Berlin, Leipzig, Wien, Stuttgart, 1908). Gives the poems in chronological order.

Sämtliche Werke. Ed. G. Baumann, 2 vols. (Stuttgart, 1954). 2nd ed., 3 vols. [including one vol. of letters] (Stuttgart, 1961).

Sämtliche Werke. Ed. H. G. Göpfert (Munich, 1954). 2nd ed. (Munich, 1958). 3rd ed. [greatly improved] (Munich, 1961). These editions are the best after Maync.

Briefe. Ed. F. Seebaß (Tübingen, 1939).

Unveröffentlichte Briefe. Ed. F. Seebaß, 2nd ed. (Stuttgart, 1945).

Eduard Mörikes Briefe. Ed. K. Fischer and R. Krauß, 2 vols. (Berlin, 1903/4). Brings some letters not contained in Seebaß. The same is true of:

Briefe. Ed. W. Zemp (Zurich, 1949).

(b) Translations:

MORGAN, B. Q. *A Critical Bibliography of German Literature in English Translation,* 2nd ed. (Stanford, 1938). Lists a number of anthologies that contain translations of Mörike poems. These anthologies were published between 1845 and 1912. More recently, translations of forty poems appeared in:

CRUICKSHANK, N. K. and CUNNINGHAM, G. F. trans. *Poems by Eduard Mörike* (London, 1959).

The old, inadequate translation of the Mozart novella was superseded by: *Mozart on the Way to Prague.* Trans. W. and C. A. Phillips

(Oxford, 1934). Translations of a few Mörike poems are also given in the appendix of the only book on the poet in English preceding this study. See the following section.

(c) Secondary studies in English:

It is the objective of this book to make Mörike's work known to those readers of world literature whose reading is limited to books in the English language. To serve this purpose, the emphasis in the following sections will be on English critical appraisals; and only those German studies will be given which are mentioned in the footnotes to the present study.

MARE, M. *Eduard Mörike: The Man and the Poet* (London, 1957). This book offers a more detailed introduction to the poet's life and his personal idiosyncrasies. A discussion of the works is interwoven but, unfortunately, the poetry is given in German, except for the few translations in the appendix.

Among the articles and dissertations, the following may be of interest:

DIECKMANN, L. "Mörike's Presentation of the Creative Process," *Journal of English and Germanic Philology*, LIII (1954).

FARRELL, R. B. "The Art of Eduard Mörike," *Proceedings of the Australian Goethe Society* (1952/53).

———. "Mörike's Classical Verse," *Publ. of the English Goethe Society*, NS 25 (1956).

———. *Mozart auf der Reise nach Prag* (Studies in German Literature 3) (London, 1960).

HEWETT-THAYER, H. H. "Mörike's Occultism and the Revision of *Maler Nolten*," *PMLA*, LXXI (1956).

———. "Traditional Technique in Mörike's *Maler Nolten*," *Germanic Review*, XXXII (1957).

IMMERWAHR, R. "Apocalyptic Trumpets: The Inception of 'Mozart auf der Reise nach Prag'," *PMLA*, LXX (1955).

———. "Narrative and 'Musical' Structure in 'Mozart auf der Reise nach Prag'," *Studies in Germanic Languages and Literatures in Memory of Fred O. Nolte*. (St. Louis, 1963).

JENNINGS, L. B. "Mörike's Grotesquery: A Post-Romantic Phenomenon," *Journal of English and Germanic Philology*, LIX (1960).

KNEISEL, J. H. *Mörike and Music*, Diss. Columbia University, 1949.

LANGE, V. "Eduard Mörike," *On Romanticism and the Art of Translation: Studies in Honor of Edwin H. Zeydel* (Princeton, 1956).

MIDDLETON, J. C. "Mörike's Moonchild." A Reading of the Poem 'Auf eine Christblume'," *Publ. of the English Goethe Society*, N. S. 28 (1959).

Selected Bibliography

PRAWER, S. S. "Mörike's 'Mein Fluß'" in *German Lyric Poetry* (London, 1952).

———. "Mignon's Revenge: A Study of Mörike's *Maler Nolten*," *Publ. of the English Goethe Society*, N. S. 25 (1956).

———. "Mörike's Second Thoughts," *Modern Philology*, LVII (1959).

———. "The Threatened Idyll: Mörike's 'Mozart auf der Reise nach Prag'," *Modern Languages*, XLIV (1963).

WILLIAMS, W. D. "Day and Night Symbolism in Some Poems of Mörike." *The Era of Goethe: Studies Presented to James Boyd* (Oxford, 1959).

(d) German works containing valuable bibliographies:

PRAWER, S. S. *Mörike und seine Leser: Versuch einer Wirkungsgeschichte* (Stuttgart, 1960). Discusses the changing appreciation of the poet. Beginning with the reactions of friends and contemporaries, Prawer traces the poet's image in the mind of readers and critics who saw in him, at times, the Swabian writer of idylls and at other times the companion of poets like Baudelaire or Poe, stressing the demonic side of his poetry. Prawer gives sixteen pages of bibliography, arranged according to dates of publication, and includes works in languages other than German or English.

MEYER, H. *Eduard Mörike*, Metzler (Stuttgart; Metzler, 1961). This volume is mainly concerned with the poet's life and the dates of origin of the major works, as well as the changing place Mörike has found in the esteem of literary critics. Each chapter of the book is followed by a list of secondary material from which the reader can find guidance in his studies of specific problems in Mörike research and interpretation.

(e) Studies in German which are mentioned in this monograph:

(1) Books and Dissertations:

ADRIAN, K. "Wege der Gestaltung in Mörikes Maler Nolten und Mozart auf der Reise nach Prag," Diss. (Münster, 1914).

GUARDINI, R. *Gegenwart und Geheimnis: Eine Auslegung von fünf Gedichten Eduard Mörikes* (Würzburg, 1957).

HÖLLERER, W. *Zwischen Klassik und Moderne* (Stuttgart, 1958).

IBEL, R. *Weltschau deutscher Dichter*, II (Hamburg, 1948).

LANDMANN, H. "Mörikes Märchen "Das Stuttgarter Hutzelmännlein" im Verhältnis zum Volksmärchen," Diss. (Berlin, 1961).

MAUTNER, F. H. *Mörikes "Mozart auf der Reise nach Prag"* (Krefeld, 1957).

MAYNC, H. *Eduard Mörike,* 3rd and 4th eds. (Stuttgart and Berlin, 1927). 5th ed. (1944). This is the most extensive biography of Mörike.

MEYER, H. *Eduard Mörike* (Stuttgart, 1950). One of two books appearing in 1950 which have attempted a re-evaluation of Mörike as a poet of great appeal to contemporary readers. Meyer's study is supported by a very close reading of the poet's works and letters, stressing Mörike's sensitivity to the undertones in nature and human relations.

NORDHEIM, W. v. "Die Einsamkeitserfahrung Mörikes und ihre Aussprache im dichterischen Werk," Diss. (Hamburg, 1954).

RUPPRECHT, G. "Mörikes Leistung als Übersetzer aus den klassischen Sprachen," Diss. (Munich, 1958).

STORZ, G. *Eduard Mörike* (Stuttgart, 1967) This most recent book on Mörike stresses Mörike's achievement in poetic forms. Following Höllerer's suggestion that Mörike shows an artistic accomplishment similar to that of the poets at the end of the nineteenth century, he retains on the other hand the characterization of Mörike as a poet who at times was not aware of the implications of his writings (p. 194) and the artistry of his forms. He particularly discusses Mörike's inspiration from dreams.

TARABA, W. F. "Vergangenheit und Gegenwart bei Mörike," Diss. (Münster, 1953).

WIESE, B. v. *Eduard Mörike* (Tübingen and Stuttgart, 1950). Emphasizes the poet's experience of dark forces and views his creation of humorous and idyllic scenes and characters as an escape, as a process of masking his sensitivity and anguish.

(2) Articles:

APPELBAUM-GRAHAM, I. "Zu Mörikes Gedicht 'Auf eine Lampe'," *Modern Language Notes,* LXVIII (1953).

BECK, A. "Mörikes 'An einem Wintermorgen, vor Sonnenaufgang,'" *Euphorion,* XLVI (1952). This article as well as the next have been published again in A. Beck, *Forschung und Deutung,* ed. U. Fülleborn (Frankfurt/Bonn, 1966), pp. 311–45.

———. 'Peregrina," *Euphorion,* XLVII (1953).

HEIDEGGER, M. and STAIGER, E. "Zu einem Vers von Mörike," *Trivium,* IX (1951).

HÖTZER, U. " 'Grata Negligentia'—'Ungestiefelte Hexameter'? Bemerkungen zu Goethes und Mörikes Hexameter," *Der Deutschunterricht,* vol. 16 (1964).

ITTENBACH, M. "Mozart auf der Reise nach Prag," *Germanisch-Romanische Monatshefte,* XXV (1937).

Selected Bibliography

KOHLSCHMIDT, W. "Wehmut, Erinnerung, Sehnsucht in Mörikes Gedicht," *Wirkendes Wort*, I (1950/51). This article was reprinted in *Form und Innerlichkeit* (Bern, 1955).

KRUMMACHER, H.-H. "Zu Mörikes Gedichten," *Jahrbuch der Deutschen Schillergesellschaft*, V (1961).

————. "Mitteilungen zur Chronologie und Textgeschichte von Mörikes Gedichten," *Ibid.*, VI (1962).

LÖSEL, F. "Mörikes Gedicht 'Im Park'," *Wirkendes Wort*, XII (1962).

MEYER, H. "Stufen der Umgestaltung des Maler Nolten," *Zeitschrift für Deutsche Philologie*, 85 (1966).

NORDHEIM, W. v. "Die Dingdichtung Eduard Mörikes," *Euphorion*, L (1956).

POLHEIM, K. K. "Der künstlerische Aufbau von Mörikes Mozartnovelle," *Euphorion*, XLVIII (1954).

SLESSAREV, H. "Der Abgrund der Betrachtung. Über den schöpferischen Vorgang bei Mörike," *German Quarterly*, XXXIV (1961).

STAIGER, E. "Mörike: 'Das verlassene Mägdlein'," *Trivium*, V (1947).

TARABA, W. F. "Eduard Mörike: 'Denk' es, o Seele!'" *Die deutsche Lyrik*, ed. B. V. Wiese (Düsseldorf, 1957) II.

WIESE, B. v. "Eduard Mörike: 'Mozart auf der Reise nach Prag'" in *Die deutsche Novelle* (Düsseldorf, 1960).

Index

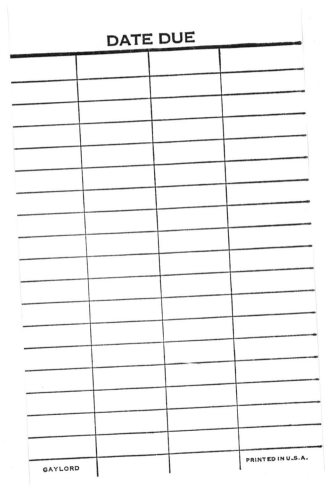